A Quick History of

DURANGO & SILVERTON NARROW GAUGE

By Duane A. Smith

ISBN 978-1-889459-12-7

Second Edition
Printed in the United States of America

WESTERN REFLECTIONS PUBLISHING COMPANY®
P. O. Box 1149
951 N. Highway 149
Lake City, CO 81235
www.westernreflectionspub.com

Table of Contents

Railroading

I've been working on the railroad
All the livelong day...

Remember that song from your youth or childhood? Does it bring back memories?

You still can hear the locomotive, smell that smoke, and even brush those cinders out of your hair with the Durango & Silverton Narrow Gauge.

I've been working on the railroad
Just to pass the time away.
Don't you hear the whistle blowing?

That lonesome whistle of folklore and legend can still be heard in the Animas Canyon.

This little volume is dedicated to those people who remember steam locomotives, have been fascinated with railroads in western history, or simply want to know more about an era that is gone. Americans fell in love with steam locomotives and railroading over a century and a half ago. At least most Americans did. Concord, Massachusetts, philosopher and writer Henry Thoreau did not. He groused that, "We do not ride on the railroad; it rides upon us." But then, Henry was not enamored with much of this "modern" world. Neither was an Ohio school board that declared, for some reason lost to history, "that railroads will lead the immortal soul down to hell."

They were both a bit out-of-step with their era.

Americans saw in the railroad the coming of age for themselves and their country. Railroading prospered for over a century, then its great age closed. Too little remains to remind us of that epoch of steam railroading. This is the story of one short line that continues to steam ahead with the vigor of its youth.

CHAPTER 1

The Land

For a hundred miles, they dominate the horizon as the traveler approaches. Rugged, majestic, beautiful—the San Juan Mountains stretch toward the sky to stand guard over southwestern Colorado. They, and the neighboring La Plata Mountains, were named by the Spanish centuries ago, when the Utes, who called this land home, roamed through the valleys and mountains. To them, these peaks were "the Shining Mountains," their summer hunting ground and home for several hundred years before the Spanish arrived.

Viewers stood in awe of what they saw and confronted, as they struggled to enter the San Juans over high passes and through deep canyons. Writers and journalists spent much time and effort trying to describe them for the uninitiated. For whatever generation that challenged them, these

As late as the 1870s, the San Juans were known as "terra incognita." (Courtesy: U.S. Geological Survey)

mountains defined the visitors' existence. Yet deep within them, the hopeful believed, were gold and silver deposits that would make the discoverers as rich as the fabled wealth of King Midas and put those Spanish conquistadors, Cortez and Pizzaro, with their golden treasures, to shame.

No one, though, would have an easy time. The San Juans challenged even the most daring and resourceful; they would not willingly give up their secrets. Isolated from settlements and main trade routes, they stood sentinel over a land that had been settled a thousand years by the long-gone Anasazi. Yet, to the Spanish explorers and later to onrushing miners, this seemed undeveloped virgin territory to be exploited for wealth and fame.

The early descriptions of it should have stopped the fainthearted and forewarned even the most adventuresome. However, there always existed the hint of the romantic and mysterious nature of this mountainous region and of wealth to be found. The gentle Catholic friars, Dominquez and Escalante, passed by in 1776, just as, far to the east, former

Pioneer photographer William H. Jackson took this photograph

5

Stony Pass and Cunningham Gulch were a main route into the San Juans. (Courtesy: U.S. Geological Survey)

British colonists declared their independence. Along the fringes of the mountains—and in the river valleys that tumbled out of the mountains—they found pastures and meadows that have "very good land for crops, with opportunities for irrigation and everything else necessary for a settlement—firewood, stone, timber, pasturage, all close at hand."

The mountains, however, they avoided, describing them as "mountains where there are very tall and straight pine trees, small oaks and several kinds of wild fruit trees." Escalante, the chronicler, continued, "They say there are veins and outcroppings of metal... The opinion formed previously by some persons from the accounts of various Indians and of some citizens of this kingdom that they were silver mines caused the mountain to be called Sierra de la Plata." Because of an illness of a member of the party, "we could not go to see the above-mentioned veins and metal-bearing rocks in the mountain, though they were not far away."

Captain John Macomb journeyed nearby in 1859, leaving this description of what he saw: "The Sierra San Juan terminated abruptly southward, standing out as a bold headland on the margin of the sea-like plateau. The altitude of its highest summits must be nearly 13,000 feet, as snow lies on them in places throughout the year." His party did not try to penetrate, but he concluded that the summits presented "very varied and picturesque outlines."

The Hayden Survey of 1874 penetrated the mountains, as, by now, prospectors and miners had. Members of the survey team left their picturesque accounts of the land. Franklin Rhoda traveled down Animas Canyon in August from the new mining camp of Animas Forks to Baker's Park, where Silverton was getting started. His vivid description gives an idea of what miners and others who challenged the San Juans had to face.

To reach Animas Forks proved no easy trip. After a mile's steep ride, Rhoda crossed a 12,540 foot pass. He wrote, "from the head of Lake Fork to the Animas. The ground up

The northern end of Baker's Park in 1875. (Courtesy: U.S. Geological Survey)

to that point is very boggy and the riding disagreeable. How the people of Saguache ever expect to bring a wagon-road up this I cannot see." Then the clouds descended.

"They never completely veiled all the peaks of the groups, but early each day began to circle about them in a restless sort of a way, like so many mighty lions about their lair.

"We even now held those peaks in awe, as there seemed to be established somewhere in their midst a regular 'manufactory of storms.' About 1 o'clock in the afternoon the clouds again came on, accompanied by hail and electric phenomena."

Undaunted, Rhoda pressed onward.

Traveling down the Animas, Rhoda observed the steep bluffs in "many places a thousand feet, nearly vertical. In some places the bluffs form the abrupt termination of what from above are seen to be sharp, rocky ridges, leading down from the peaks." Eventually reaching Baker's Park, he described what he saw.

"The great and important feature of this region is the far-famed Baker's Park. Small in area and quite unimportant in itself, it would be utterly disregarded if situated in other parts of Colorado; but, located as it is, surrounded on all sides by the most rugged mountains in the Territory, if not in the whole Rocky Mountain system, this little area of flat land becomes an object of curiosity and interest. But not till one has crossed over the several passes leading out of it can he feel a proper regard for this little spot, so carefully guarded by nature from the invasion of man." In this beautiful park sat "the new town of Silverton, at present containing about a dozen houses."

To the south lay more problems. "At the lower end of the park the Animas swings around toward the southeast, and for about seven miles cuts a most terrific canon, ranging in depth from 2,000 to 4,500 feet, through quartzite rock almost as hard as steel." Baker's Park was isolated, as Rhoda well knew. "First, let me say that the ruggedness of the Great Canon below the park is such that travel through it must long be a matter of great difficulty." The trail around it, he concluded, "is the roughest and most dangerous of any leading out of the park."

The other "roads" were not much better. A. D. Wilson was also with the Hayden Survey that season, and he left this description of the Lake Fork trail that Rhoda had taken. The road would take considerable expense to get "a very good grade, until nearing the pass, where the mountains rise quite abruptly, and it will be very difficult to construct a good road over this pass, as it is quite steep on either side." The road from Del Norte, via Cunningham Creek, seemed to him the "most practicable route at present," but the grade was steep and rocky and a loaded wagon could not cross it.

Traveler and writer, Ernest Ingersoll, was nearly carried away when he visited the San Juans a few years later.

"Overhead, tower the rosy and gleaming monuments of that old time 'when the gods were young and the world was new'—cliffs rising so steeply that only here and there can they be climbed, and studded with domes and pinnacles so slender and lofty that, under our unsteady glance, they seem to totter and swim vaguely through the azure concave."

He agreed with Rhoda about Silverton, "its founders preempted almost the only site for a town of any consequence in the whole region. Engulfed amid lofty peaks, a little park lies as level as a billiard-table."

These, then, were the obstacles that prospectors, miners, road builders, town dreamers, freighters, travelers, and railroad engineers had to confront in the challenge to open the silver and gold wealth of the San Juans and bring permanent settlement.

Frank Fossett wrote in 1876, just at the dawning of permanent settlement in these isolated rugged mountains, "The San Juan country—a region that bids fair to surpass all others on the globe in enormous size and length of its silver bearing veins—a section that remained a *terra incognita* through all the years that other Colorado mining districts were discovered and developed."

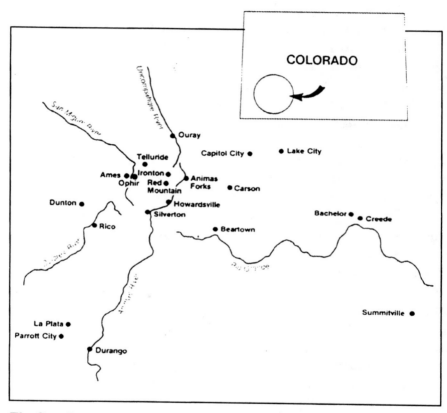

The San Juan mining region, 1860-1914. (Courtesy: Author)

The Problem

A mining district needs three things to be successful: rich and plentiful ore bodies, money for investment and development, and the best possible transportation. The San Juans had bountiful ore deposits, but for decades ran chronically short of the capital and confronted only slightly better than marginal transportation. As a result, it was a district that seemed destined to be "always a bridesmaid, never a bride."

San Juaners spent many long winter hours dreaming about—and discussing and cussing—transportation. As the highest mining district in the United States, the San Juans demanded year-round, fast, and economical transportation. Until that was achieved, it would never attain the destiny that seemed to be ordained for the region.

Investors would not be lured until transportation improved. They might be intrigued by stories of rich strikes, and

The San Juans are the highest mining region in the United States:
Highland Mary Mine. (Courtesy: U.S. Geological Survey)

11

*Even placer mining was hard, difficult work. These miners were in
Borens Gulch.* (Courtesy: U.S. Geological Survey)

maybe even the rugged scenery, but they would arrive more
easily and comfortably at their destination when transportation drastically improved. Descriptions such as the following
did little to entice outsiders to make the journey. "The San
Juans were beautiful, that could not be denied, but they were
also...abrupt and broken, with an average elevation of 13,000
feet above the sea, with some of their peaks reaching the altitude of 14,500 feet. The scenery of such a section must necessarily verge nearer to the sublime than any known in the world.
Nature must have been in wild riot to have produced such a
'wreck of matter' as is here found."

The writer took a little "artistic license," but picturing the
San Juans as " a scene of abandoned nature" did not generally
lure financiers and investors into their isolated vastness.

Such was the lure of mineral riches, however, that such
problems were initially ignored, as miners rushed to tap the
wealth they knew awaited them over the next mountain or
deep in unnamed canyons. Gold fever, silver fever—or what-

ever mineral fever—proves a powerful force. One need only find a mine, and his or her fortune rested assured. Or so it seemed to the uninitiated. Mining seemed the royal road to wealth, to get rich "without working." The uninitiated were naive; they would find out the truth eventually.

The Spanish had come in the eighteenth century and departed. Isolation, unhappy Utes, Spanish colonial policy, and mountainous terrain defeated them. Not until the Pike's Peak gold rush of 1859 did interest again turn prospectors and miners to the central Rockies. Charles Baker (hence, the name of the park) and party arrived in 1860. He proclaimed it a second California, a placer mining paradise; it was not. Yet, in 1861, a mini-rush of the hopeful braved long miles and mountains to reach his park. They left discouraged, and the San Juans were proclaimed a "humbug" by even Colorado newspapers. They were not, but it would take nearly a decade to overcome that season's misadventures.

In 1869 and 1870, prospectors again probed the San Juans. Then came encouraging reports of gold strikes. Again, the people came. Unlike the sixties, this rush was based upon lode or hard rock mining, a more stable proposition than placer operations. By 1872, the rush was in full swing, with reports of three-to-six-foot veins of silver (not the initially reported gold) being found. The San Juans proved a mineral treasure box, with gold, silver, lead, zinc, and other metals being mined before the end of the mining era. Then, as now, gold and silver remained the glamour metals, the ones that excited men and women.

Initially, the miners came into the mountains in the late spring and left with the first snows. By 1874, however, permanent settlements were taking root. These were the ones that the men of the Hayden Survey commented on as they pushed through the San Juans. Once these settlements evolved, the costly and burdensome chore of leaving every winter could be avoided, and mining would have the base to expand on a year-round basis. A new era had dawned.

By mid-decade, these valleys and mountains would

San Juan trails were an adventure in the 1870s as William Henry Jackson showed. (Courtesy: U.S. Geological Survey)

never again be uninhabited; miners moving into them would discover camps, mining districts, and mining laws awaiting them. Like mining elsewhere, this emerged as an urban west. The miners depended upon others to provide them services, while they toiled in their mines. They, after all, at least expected to have gold and silver to pay for such services. Almost on the heels of the miners came those folks who would "mine the miners." These urbanites became the foundation for the little camps and towns that sprang up in the San Juans in the 1870s and 1880s.

The San Juans had many miles yet to go, but even the most pessimistic would have to concur that they had come a far distance since the Baker excitement in 1860-61. Yet, despite optimism, miner and camp dweller alike faced a problem—poor transportation. What caused it was not difficult to discover—isolation, elevation, and weather. The inadequate, seasonal transportation that existed caused problems, irritating nearly everybody: a higher cost of living, scarcity of supplies in the winter, slow delivery of needed goods and equipment, investors unwilling to put up with the trials and tribulations of trying to reach the San Juans, and lethargic growth.

Comments about the problem and its impacts appeared from the very beginning. April 1872 mining, it was reported, was carried on in "a crude state owing to want of proper machinery for reducing, crushing and refining." Proper machinery—or machinery of any kind—could not be brought in over the primitive trails. Remember what the Hayden party, as mentioned earlier, thought of those trails when they struggled over them two years later. They obviously had not improved.

Noted photographer, William Henry Jackson, a member of the Hayden party in 1874, commented in his diary after going over Stony Pass, "What can possess those people we pass to go into that place this time of year [September]? Passed burro trains & wagons. Smashed up wagon there..." Miner Alfred Camp fought his way over the trail into Cunningham Gulch, "This experience will hardly be forgotten as for several hours we scrambled and slid as best we could to get down—fortunately without breaking our necks."

Of the Stony Pass route, Camp concluded it to be "almost an impassable road winding upward." While it was the only route which loaded wagons could use, the wagons had to be "snubbed down by ropes or chains," using trees as the anchor. It was, he ended, "as hard to get an empty wagon out as to bring a loaded one in."

A letter from San Juaner W. B. Dickinson to Denver's *Rocky Mountain News* (November 1, 1874) summarized the problem very well:

> One begins to curse the roads immediately after he leaves Antelope Park, and, though rough roads *have* been experienced before, at the summit of the range roads that are—not roads at all—are encountered.

Transporting goods to the mines by pack train was costly and time-consuming. (Courtesy: U.S. Geological Survey)

Old-time miner, Rasmus Hanson, who arrived in 1876 and stayed, had this to say about the road from Ouray to Mineral Point that year: a "man risked his life on it. It was not safe to ride a horse over it. When slippery, it was unsafe to walk over."

As poor as these roads must have been, it was worse not to have an outlet. The editor of Rico's *Dolores News,* in August 1879, complained that "there is not a marked trail thus far leading into the camp, nor a wagon road of any size or dimensions yet constructed." Soon after, Ricoites cheered when they gained a wagon road outlet to the south. A road "is what every camp and district want and must have." The editor was absolutely right, but once one appeared, travelers demanded improvements or a better road.

Rico was a new community, but older camps suffered, even after several years of habitation. One of the earliest settlements, four-year-old Silverton, the *Rocky Mountain News* pointed in June 1877, "suffered greatly for want of roads." The only practical route ran through New Mexico. There were other ways in summer, "but summers are very short." Summers were very short and winters raised the cost of transportation alarmingly, when mule trains could not even move through the snow.

It was bad enough when San Juaners bemoaned such conditions. Far worse was when outsiders understood them and pointed them out. That was terrible for the local image and endangered the future. Hence, when even a newspaper, as far away as the *New York Times* (November 3, 1876), noted that "the best way and almost only way" to reach mining camps beyond Lake City "is by pack animals," the situation looked bleak. The respected mining journal, the *Engineering and Mining Journal,* remarked in December 1877 that ore transportation in southwestern Colorado depended so much on animal transportation, yet the districts were "so poorly equipped with good trails and wagon roads" that the situation proved devastating to one and all. That bleak situation demanded reversing.

The time had come for improvement. San Juaners knew it. It was not, the editor of Lake City's *Silver World* (September 18, 1875) concluded, smelters that the San Juans needed at the moment. "The greater and more immediate want is the necessity of thoroughfares and highways."

Too often, all they read were comments like, the Mineral Point trail "is sadly in need of repair."

It was not that the San Juaners did not work at it. They did. Reports of roads being built or improved appeared almost with the first newspaper accounts. Complaints surfaced at the same time. Colorado and the local counties did not have the finances to build a needed transportation network. Therefore, it was not long before private enterprise stepped in, building toll roads. Saguache's Otto Mears came to fame building roads to and into the neighboring San Juans. Even he did not escape criticism about high tolls and poor condition of the thoroughfares. Most of the toll roads eventually came under county control.

Nor were San Juaners enamored with the prospect of paying to rush into the mines. One of them admitted that "all kinds of schemes were used to avoid payment of the toll." Some folks simply said they did not have the money and "got by with a promise to pay afterward." Much of the mining West was built on promises and hope, so why not toll payments!

Roads and trails were simply not the ultimate answer. Natural advantages, rich mineral deposits, a promising future all would go for naught, if transportation did not improve and cheapen. What they needed was easy; getting it proved the difficult part. Mining engineer and San Juan booster Thomas Comstock wrote, as the decade came to an end in December 1879, "the coming railroad is of vast importance to the region."

Comstock could not have been more correct. The railroad was the answer, and it was coming. Colorado's own Denver & Rio Grande had its eye on the San Juan region and its most promising silver future.

CHAPTER 3

The Answer

The railroad. The Iron Horse. Americans fell in love with it, almost from its very first smoky appearance. The iron rails and iron horse solved, for the nineteenth century, two pressing problems—distance and isolation. Having crossed the Appalachian Mountains, Americans left behind the ease of ocean travel. They now found themselves confronting those twin problems on the prairies and plains. Beyond loomed the mountains. The answer, the railroad.

They took the railroad "to their bosom," as they were wont to say. European countries were generally too small, or caught up in national rivalries, to get as excited over the potential and possibilities of this new form of transportation.

American railroading and achievements had been spectacular, even before pioneers ventured across the Missouri

Idealized drawing of pioneers moving west before the coming of the railroad. (Courtesy: Author)

Laying track on the Colorado was much easier than in the mountains.
(Courtesy: Author)

River. They had, in fact, been transforming America before the Civil War threatened to split it apart. The railroad idea came from England, but Americans developed it into the defining mode of transportation.

The Baltimore and Ohio Railroad opened a few miles to traffic in 1830, and an era dawned. Ten years later, the total railroad trackage in the United States had reached 2818 miles. By 1860, mileage topped 30,000, and a town without railroad connections was poor indeed. New cars, bigger engines, heavier rails, the telegraph, better road beds, and a host of other things made traveling faster, safer, and more comfortable. The railroads impacted all segments of American life, from agriculture to industry to urbanization. This was no more clearly shown than in coal mining. Coal was profitable freight—it was the preferred fuel and easily transported. Railroads came to own mines and transported coal everywhere along their lines.

Railroads rolled west with the pioneers. Texas (1852),

California (1852), and Kansas (1855) laid rails, but the big hope persisted, a transcontinental line that would connect east with west. Crossing unsettled territory, this line would have to be built with assistance from the federal government. However, like so many other matters, the sectional/ slavery dispute killed any chance of construction. Not until the Civil War broke out did the government at last take action. Finally, in 1862, a transcontinental bill passed Congress; track laying slowly started. The post-war years saw construction really boom, as the Central Pacific raced eastward and the Union Pacific westward. They would meet at Promontory, Utah, on May 10, 1869.

Meanwhile, the 1859 Pike's Peak gold rush brought settlement to future Colorado. The buoyant and enthusiastic optimism that shaped those years called for railroad connections as soon as possible. With a sparse population, insufficient local capital, and a federal government caught up in war, little except talk would be accomplished.

The first two territorial governors, William Gilpin and John Evans, never let the dream die. Speaking to the first session of the legislature, Gilpin, in his usual flowery, soaring way, predicted that the great American Dream of a "CONTINENTAL RAILWAY" was about to be fulfilled. It must pass through the center of Colorado, he forecast. "Our territory will be bisected East and West, by the grandest work of all time...to draw the travel and commerce of all the nations, and all the continents of the world."

Evans, an interminable railroad booster, proved almost more enthusiastic. One of his first acts as governor was to initiate a survey of Berthoud Pass as a possible route. Evans described the pass—it looked to "have been designed by the Great Master Mechanic" as a railroad route. It did not provide the needed solution, even though Evans speculated gold might be discovered while digging a tunnel under it.

Alas, the transcontinental route went over gentler South Pass, barely touching Colorado at Julesburg in the far northeastern corner of the territory. Equally as damaging, the

Union Pacific started the rival town of Cheyenne in newly formed Wyoming Territory. Dismayed, but not down, Evans and other Denver "movers and shakers" built their own railroad, the Denver Pacific, to connect with the transcontinental.

Finally, in 1870, Denver's railroad "cup of blessings" filled to the brim. The Denver Pacific was completed, and the Kansas Pacific reached town. Cheyenne's threat evaporated, and Den-

William Jackson Palmer in the early 1870s. (Courtesy: Author)

ver gained its railroad connections to the east and west. The decade-old dream had been realized.

Dreams never quite satisfy everyone, and other folks had their own dreams, too. None would be more important to Colorado and the San Juans than that of a man who came with the Kansas Pacific, William Jackson Palmer. Thirty-four-year-old Palmer had learned railroading before the war with the Pennsylvania Railroad. During the Civil War, he had risen to the rank of brigadier general of volunteers and, after Appomattox, cast his fortunes with railroading as the

22

key to success in the West. He was joined by a lot of other former enlisted men and officers, who provided the backbone of railroad construction across the Great Plains.

Palmer became treasurer, then secretary-treasurer, of the Kansas Pacific. The West, he correctly foresaw, offered enormous opportunities for enterprising individuals who acted as agents for eastern capitalists. While being in general charge of the Kansas Pacific survey in 1867–68, Palmer fell in love with the southwest and particularly southern Colorado—a land, he felt, which held great agricultural and mining opportunities.

Cutting himself loose from the Kansas Pacific, Palmer struck out on his own. He had a plan and went to Denver to find support. His plan was simple, build a north/south feeder line along the mountains to tap the east/west transcontinental lines and open the land in between. This seemed the perfect place to start. From Denver, his railroad would go to El Paso, Texas, and eventually into Mexico.

Like John Evans, Palmer agreed that "Colorado without railroads is comparatively worthless." Unfortunately for the young man, Denver's capital and enterprise were tied up in the Denver Pacific. Undaunted, Palmer set out to raise funds in the eastern states and in England. He would not be stopped.

His plan to use the narrow gauge (three feet) rather than the standard 4 foot, 8½ inch gauge was not revolutionary, but it stood him in good stead in a few years. The slender veteran was a complex dreamer and hard-headed businessman. He would not only build a railroad, but would establish towns along the way, open mines, and encourage ranchers and farmers to come. He did not plan to take advantage of his workers; he dreamed that "it would be quite a little family." That was not all. "Everybody should be looked after to see that there was no distress among the workmen and their families—and schools should be put for them and bath-houses." It did not work out quite as he planned, but the concept was unusual.

The first section of the Denver & Rio Grande opened in October 1871, from Denver to Palmer's Colorado Springs. Dubbed "Little London," because of the number of English that eventually settled there, Colorado Springs would be his pride and joy, and his home. It proved a rousing success, with nearly 800 residents within a few months. Colorado Springs soon became a cosmopolitan, planned community, probably the most cultured in the territory, that emerged as a tourist, health, education, and business center.

Palmer and his backers now made plans to duplicate that success all along the D&RG line. They built on southward to the southern Colorado coal fields. The Rio Grande needed coal for fuel for their locomotives, and there was a ready Colorado market for car loads of the "black diamond." Like back east, railroads soon found themselves in the coal business, developing coal mines and mining camps.

Despite the fact that communities along the line needed the railroad, the D&RG was not always loved. The railroad would build next to a town, then ask for terms—land, money, stock purchase—and, if none came forth, the company would start a rival town that had D&RG connections. Pueblo, Trinidad, Canon City, and others felt the pressure. This did not endear Palmer or his railroad to many southern Coloradans. When a rival appeared, the Atchison, Topeka and Santa Fe Railroad, it would be welcomed.

Then the national depression of 1873 dried up funding and stopped the D&RG, as well as many other railroads, in its tracks. As the depression lifted in 1877–78, Leadville exploded on the scene. Other towns might have to bow and scrape to get a railroad, but not Leadville. Railroads fought to reach it. The D& RG and Santa Fe both attempted to build up Royal Gorge and ended up hiring gunfighters, bringing in high-priced experts, spending much money, and, finally, fighting it out in court. Palmer almost lost control of his railroad before the case was finished. The end result changed the Denver & Rio Grande's destiny.

Denver & Rio Grande locomotive at Chama, New Mexico, on way to Durango. (Courtesy: Colorado Historical Society)

Palmer gained the Royal Gorge route but had to give up his New Mexico dreams, which went to the Santa Fe, along with Raton Pass. For the short run, the D&RG gained. It now turned into the mountains and their mining districts. Leadville would never be Palmer's alone, however; other lines planned to tap that bonanza, too.

He might not dominate Leadville's silver boom; nevertheless, other districts waited out there, including the tempting San Juans. For the first railroad to reach the region, the rewards promised to be great. One of Palmer's lifelong friends, Dr. William Bell, advised him about the San Juans: "Indeed, the trade of these counties had yielded to the freighters and stage coach proprietors that carried during the past year, enough money to enable a railroad to either district to pay from its net receipts 7 per cent interest on bonds to the amount of $20,000 per mile of road." Bell went on to say that "such a condition of things is exceptional in Western States." Palmer was hooked. Writing Bell, he said that

Leadville and the San Juans "will put D&RG on a stock dividend paying basis."

Regardless of the railroad's sagging financial condition, the first segment over La Veta Pass was completed in 1876, even before the fight for Royal Gorge commenced. Construction moved by jumps and starts. On to Salida and Alamosa in 1878, then, in 1880, to Antonito and beyond. Always ahead beckoned the San Juans.

The early part had been the easiest. The San Juan branch, as it was called, continued on. As it moved up Cumbres Pass to Chama, New Mexico, the railroad faced a killer schedule when it encountered high passes and torturous grades. At one point, to cover a half mile distance, the D&RG built two-and-a-half miles of track, trestle, and embankment. One mile of that alone cost $140,000. Then there was always winter weather, and it proved hard to keep workers. Regardless of high wages, they tended to desert and race on to the mines.

Despite construction difficulties and high costs, the San Juans continued to beckon. As a newspaper correspondent wrote, "The railroad heard the tales of the prospectors and miners and looked westward." Ahead lay "the new land of promise."

As Palmer and his railroad labored onward, San Juaners anxiously wished he would hurry along a bit faster. The editor of Lake City's *Silver World* (September 30, 1876) observed, "That there will be a railroad in this country within two years, hardly anybody who knows anything about the matter doubts, the question being as to the line and the direction." They correctly guessed that Palmer would come up to the Animas Valley, past Animas City, and then tackle the canyon beyond. Actually, they did not care if the D&RG arrived or someone else. There were other "paper railroads" announcing this or that scheme, but none came near to reality.

CHAPTER 4

The Railroad Does It All

Two little villages awaited the coming of the iron horse with unbounded expectations. Nestled far north, near the headwaters of the Animas River, Silverton knew its long awaited mining "promised millennium" finally neared. Forty miles south, as the crow flies, the farming village of Animas City held almost as high hopes. Both believed that their day of destiny dawned, as the surveyors and track layers approached. Silvertonians and Animas Citians enthusiastically waited their noisy, smoky salvation.

They were right about it in some respects. The coming of the Denver & Rio Grande changed forever the history of the beautiful Animas Valley. Development, in all respects, followed the iron rail. Silverton's major mining era was dawning. Thanks to the D&RG, and three other little narrow gauge lines, Silverton would soon become the "narrow gauge capital" of Colorado. Alas, Animas City's fate proved much different.

Mining gave birth to Animas City, just as it had to Silverton, although no mines could be seen from its dusty streets. The nearest mining district lay due west, some twenty roundabout miles in the isolated La Plata Mountains. Locals, however, could drive their teams and wagons up to some nearby coal seams and dig out a winter's supply of fuel. Despite such a windfall, Animas City remained a farming/ranching community that serviced the needs of miners in the San Juans and La Platas.

Animas City's location along the west bank of the Animas River provided a vital, steady water supply, and the growing season of ninety to one hundred days far surpassed anything in the mountainous San Juan mining country. Miners in the San Juan had the money to pay for their agricultural products; this provided a perfect combination. Such an unusual development for a farming community provided an economic windfall. Typically, they did not have such an accessible market quite so quickly.

Animas City also benefited from mining in another way. With nearby hot springs and a milder climate, according to the *Dolores News* (November 15, 1879), "Animas City is the winter resort for hundreds of denizens of the San Juan." They left the mountains, as "soon as the snow begins to fly," for a "jolly good time during the long winter season with amusements, pleasures, enjoyments and pastimes." Just how the little community provided such a mecca, the writer, unfortunately, failed to mention. However, he was right, there was an "abundance of farm products."

While it might have deemed itself a city, Animas City only mustered 286 folks for the 1880 census taker. Westerners liked to tag "city" onto their village names. It made them look impressive on the map for visitors and the uninitiated. Despite its size, the village was putting on "metropolitan" airs. It had a church, school, hotel, an attorney, several general merchants, and blacksmiths and a saloon. The residents had incorporated in October 1878 and awaited what they considered would be their coming of age. So did the rather large number of men, who listed themselves as builders in an 1879 business census.

Animas Citians were generally older, and more likely to be married (with their families with them), than their neighboring Silvertonians. Animas City reflected a typical, slow-growing farming/family community. Contemporaries might be found everywhere on the Great Plains and the prairies of Iowa and Illinois.

The seasons came and went, with optimism undergirding everything. Nothing was more exciting than the Fourth of July. Colorado was three years old in 1879, when Animas City put on its festivities. The day opened with an anvil chorus, all the blacksmiths hammering away, and was heralded by "pop-crackers" throughout. Then came the traditional speeches, two in this case—one by "our preacher, another by the ex-village schoolmaster." Music by "ladies, with an organ accompaniment" ended the ceremony. Lemonade for all and races took place in the afternoon, followed by a "hop in the evening" that concluded the day.

That joyous fourth had hardly faded into history, when even better news arrived from the south. The D&RG was coming. Survey crews were coming near on their way to Silverton. The future of Animas City could not have loomed brighter. Then, the recently elected city fathers made a fatal mistake. They misread history.

The D&RG, following its typical pattern, would come to Animas City, if and when the community met its conditions. Perhaps because the village also had the possibility of having a military post next door, the councilmen refused to meet the unspecified terms the railroad demanded. The troops were bivouacking across the river to prevent a threatened "Ute Uprising." That development came because of trouble a week's travel north at the White River reservation, that ended with the killing of agent Nathan Meeker. The Southern Utes remained peaceful. That did not stop local worries and fears.

Making the best of the situation, Animas City merchants envisioned a permanent post, right next door, with government contracts, jobs, and a host of benefits. With the railroad coming and the military already here, the greatest financial windfall the young community had ever experienced seemed near at hand.

Mark Twain once wrote, "The castle-building habit, the daydream habit—how it grows!" Animas City was caught right in the midst of it, the time for "castles" seemed now. Still, the best laid plans can go astray. First, the army decided not to build a fort next to a settlement with such "attractions" as Animas City seemed to afford. It was not the fault of the locals. The army had a policy about not building posts near urban areas. More crucial to the future towered the outcome of the railroad negotiations.

The courtship turned rocky. Animas City terribly misjudged its importance and stood pat, a not unusual position

Animas City made a mistake, and the Denver & Rio Grande never stopped there. (Courtesy: U.S. Geological Survey)

taken by western towns. The winter months froze negotiations, and spring did not thaw them out. As early as December 1879, the "D&RG people are busy taking up town sites" and coal lands. It was even rumored that they were laying out grounds for shops. By May 1880, it was reported that businesses were planning to open in "the new town of Durango on the Rio Animas," when the D&RG reached the area. A visitor already called Durango "quite beautifully located."

Animas City's *Southwest* hurled defiance, "What the 'new town of Durango' is to be or not to be, God and the D&RG Railroad only know." The railroad took sole responsibility. It did not need help from the deity in what was about to happen.

Silverton's *La Plata Miner,* December 20, 1879, had correctly read the future. The new town, to be located two miles down river from Animas City, "will knock the stuffing out of the present town, yet it will be a good thing for us all, and especially our San Juan neighbors."

The result doomed Animas City. First, it lost out in the post selection; Fort Lewis was located sixteen miles southwest of the community. Then, by midsummer, it was more than obvious that the railroad intended to fulfill its threat and start a new town two miles south along the banks of the Animas. Locals also lost the choice coal sites to the onrushing D&RG management, who eyed them from the start. They needed that fuel, as did the miners in the mountains.

Animas City kept up a brave front. A local reporter to the *La Plata Miner* (October 9, 1880) described it as a "lively place," with improvements "going on and not a house for rent in the place."

Having misread history, Animas City would eventually become just that—history. The railroad came and it went. A traveler in Durango could buy a ticket to Silverton, Denver, or almost any place a railroad ran, but not to Animas City. The D&RG did not stop there. Rallying, the town overcame the initial shock of railroad and rival; nonetheless, it never recovered. It became a bedroom community for its larger and thriving neighbor. In 1947, Animas City voters and Durangoans chose to unite, which they did officially the next year.

The Denver & Rio Grande had claimed its first victim in the San Juans. It might have failed with its policy, when threatening other towns, but here it proved dramatically successful. The railroad officials without delay set about to build the town that would change the region forever—Durango.

Durango. The name rings western, but it is really a Basque word, whose meaning has aroused antiquarians for decades—waterville, meeting place, water, or town were possibilities. It mattered little, then or now. Durango was going to get the railroad, and that was the all important issue. It can be said that it was named after Durango, Mexico, which was named after Durango in Spain.

The first survey stake was driven on September 13, 1880. By Christmas, with some of the construction crews of

Durango in the spring of 1881 awaited the coming of the train. (Courtesy: Author)

the oncoming railroad wintering in town, Durango had an estimated population of more than 2,000. Enthusiastic boosters, of which Durango would have many over the years, placed the figure at 10,000. It mattered little—it was already nearly ten times larger than rival Animas City. Old-timers were already saying that "a pleasanter place" to spend the winter did not exist in Colorado.

It was a planned community, again a D&RG goal. Main Avenue would be the business district. Up the bench, east from the riverside, would be Second Avenue, standing as buffer between the church and residential street, which was the Boulevard (present Third Avenue), and the noise, dust, and commotion of the business heart of the "Denver of Southern Colorado." Durangoans always have thought big!

Louisa Weinig arrived in November, as Durango was in the midst of its initial construction boom. It was the urban west at its birth.

I shall never forget the excitement and noise going on as we entered the town....Very few houses and stores were yet completed, but the noise made by wagons and teams and men, and by the saws and hammers of the builders proved that houses would soon take the place of tents, which were living and business quarters at that time. Boom it became, with residential lots selling for $25 and up and corner business lots for as high as $1,000.

Caroline Romney, Durango's first newspaper editor, arrived with a flourish in late December. This land "flowing with milk and honey," and "seamed with silver and gold and floored with coal," would be the "new wonder in the Southwest." As Durango boomed, La Plata County prospered as never before.

Caroline took time from promoting and defending her new home (according to her—Leadville, Silverton, and Denver were highly jealous) to take stock of the town in March. She found a strong business community of specialized stores—bakeries, news depots, meat markets, dry good stores, shoe shops, drug stores, groceries, hardware stores, saddle shops, and a bank—as well as those a visitor might expect to find in a six-month-old western town—hotels, restaurants, livery stables, blacksmiths, saloons, stage lines, real estate firms, and lodging houses. All told, 134 business houses had located in Durango. Twenty of these were saloons, the start of Durango's Red Light district.

She counted twelve lawyers, three physicians, two dressmakers, a tailor, and one church (with two other congregations forming) and two weekly, and one daily, newspapers. One had come down from Animas City *(Southwest),* as had the bank and several other businesses. Such was the fate of slightly more than five-year-old Animas City, when it was challenged by the "magic city."

Rapid growth and instant boom separated Durango from the more typical urban pattern of the Animas Cities of the world. Some mining towns grew that fast, Leadville, for instance, but Silverton and its neighbors had not achieved such a status so quickly.

It might have seemed wonderful to Caroline and the other boosters, but it was still a rough-edged, unwashed community, sitting in a beautiful mountain rimmed and river-sided site. So far, all that could be said was that Durango had lived up to the forecast, "She is bound to boom."

Not all had the vision and optimism of Caroline. Mrs. Hubertine Pulvermiller was not impressed, even when she arrived two years later. "I was disappointed in Durango ... I had expected to see a grassy spot covered with trees, instead there was only scrub oak, sage and service berry brush, and only a few trees." Estelle Camp, who arrived as the bride of banker Alfred Camp in 1883, was not enthralled either. Not only did it not look like her green and well watered New England home, it did not act like it either. There were, she remembered, a "scarcity of women on the streets; one infrequently met a woman or an old man." There seemed to be, this cultured New Englander remarked, only "two extremes of social life—the cultured, well-educated, traveled class" and the "wild and wooly followers of mining and lumber camps and cattle ranges."

Caroline would leave after a year and a half; Estelle stayed the rest of her life and came to love her home. Like her, the town overcame early problems and developed into the commercial, transportation, and mining center the railroad organizers had forecast.

The D&RG did not even arrive until the summer of 1881. By then, it had sealed the fate of one community, given birth to another, and was equally awaited by a third. Not only that, its leadership had purchased Silverton's best smelter and taken its machinery to Durango. Silverton's ever optimistic *La Plata Miner* (October 16, 1880) did not yield an inch. Others might be crestfallen, but not its editor. "The removal is not fraught with injury and disaster to Silverton and vicinity," he predicted, as "is feared by many." Even expectant Silverton was learning that the railroad gave and the railroad also took away. At the moment, he wrote, not a rail existed within a hundred miles of this mining town.

The "tiger also stalked in hearts" of Durangoans as well. Right from the very first, they planned to become the county seat. They now demanded an election to move the La Plata County seat and promptly took it away, in late 1881, from the declining mining camp of Parrott City, a small mining camp at the mouth of La Plata Canyon. It, too, was doomed. Like Silverton, Durangoans knew the coming of the railroad would bring even more benefits. They had not yet seen the other side of the equation.

Considering all these events, the jury was still out on the hoped for benefits. Had the *La Plata Miner* been right back in 1879? Would the coming of the D&RG "be a good thing for us all, and especially our San Juan neighbors"?

Silverton knew that the railroad would turn its fortune around.
(Courtesy: U.S. Geological Survey)

CHAPTER 5

Marvelous Construction and Engineering Feat

The Denver & Rio Grande finally reached Durango in July 1881. Unfortunately, some excited early arrivals had built their buildings where the railroad right-of-way existed. Now profits had to give way to practicality. The railroad's attorney told these eager aspirants that they had to "at once commence the removal of business houses." They needed to be removed immediately for the railroad to move on toward its Silverton goal. Caroline Romney remarked that they were "very reluctant to go," but "nevertheless they must." Meanwhile, Durango celebrated, with the *Durango Herald's* bold headline calling it an "EVENTFUL DAY."

It was that, to be sure. People from all parts of the San Juan region crowded into Durango on August 4–6. A parade, races, and a baseball game (Durango defeated Silverton 10–3), highlighted festivities, closed by a "grand hop." That the special excursion train was delayed by washed out tracks eighty miles from Durango did not discourage the participants. They waited for the speeches and other ceremonies the next day.

Once the railroad reached Durango and the appropriate ceremonies were conducted, the Denver and Rio Grande workers hurried on toward their goal—Silverton and the San Juan mines. It had been a long time arriving at this point. Now grading and bridging moved northward in August. Track laying moved ahead in October 1881. Silvertonians could hardly wait, but they would for one more snowy season.

The railroad soon found out firsthand about San Juan winters, and this one proved to be mild. In December, construction stopped at the little stage station hamlet of Rockwood, eighteen miles north of Durango. Described a few years later by traveler and writer Ernest Ingersoll as a "lively village" in a "secluded yet picturesque" setting,

Rockwood entered its "fifteen minutes of fame." It briefly served as the end of tracks, with piles of railroad material there, especially when the railroad to Durango opened for business in January. The *Durango Record,* February 14, 1882, forecast that "as a business point it will be second to none in the State in the early spring."

Rockwood, for a brief moment, enjoyed prosperity. (Courtesy: Colorado Historical Society)

The spritely burg already promoted itself as having "a number of first class business lots" available at reasonable prices. Rockwood, "terminus of the Denver & Rio Grande R.R.," reserved no lots; it was a "first come, first served" basis. Its founders dreamed the dream, but like many other western communities, the dream vanished with the coming of dawn. The railroad to Silverton only paused here, then passed through. Rockwood, on the mountainous road to Silverton, served as the stage terminus until the railroad reached Baker's Park, ending much of the traffic. For a longer while, Rockwood was the stage connection with Rico, the Dolores Valley, Ophir, and Telluride, to the west over the mountains.

Rockwood had a population of about a hundred in the mid-1880s, a post office, school, general store, saloon, and other businesses. It became, for a brief time, a popular picnic site for Animas City and Durango folks. Rockwood's heyday passed, however, when the Rio Grande Southern reached Rico and Telluride in 1891, ending the need for a stage line and toll road. Then, Rockwood's day slipped away. The town's population declined to half by 1900.

This first stage of construction out of Durango had been the easy part. Ahead lay the seemingly unconquerable Animas Canyon, a gorge already renowned as almost impassable for people, let alone wagons or a railroad.

The *La Plata Miner* watched the progress and problems with unabated interest. Simply surveying the line had caused difficulties. Back in 1879, the surveying party working on locating the line through the canyon had faced its trials. The "slow, difficult task," the paper reported on October 25, had been "one attended with some danger." Surveyors dangled down "on ropes over the walls of the canyon in order to get a level." Despite all this, by November, excited Silvertonians greeted the crews as they camped south of town.

This inspired the editor of the *Miner* to write an editorial about the benefits ready to be showered on Silverton with the advent of the railroad. The Rio Grande offered a Thanksgiving cornucopia. It would "give us":

Uninterrupted communication with the outside world year round

Greatly cheapen the freight rates and render them uniform year round

Allow mines to ship low grade ore at a profit

Lower the cost of mining

Make possible the erecting of extensive works [smelter] by cheapening the cost of freighting heavy machinery and supplies

"In fact, it is impossible to estimate the great advantage in every way the completion of this road will be to our camp."

The advantages, however, would not be all one-sided.

The "plucky road" would be coming into a "rich mining district," with half-developed mines, through a group of fertile valleys. This would "prove a rich harvest."

Unable to contain himself further, the editor soared into euphoria. When the D&RG reached Silverton, "perhaps next year," that would be "the beginning of the boom for this country." The town would "not cease growing for a hundred years to come." All San Juan communities and their counterparts everywhere showed such fervor and intensity at the mention of the iron horse.

Next year would come, but with it no train. Rumors, always rumors, raced up the canyon into the mountains. In December 1880, it was "understood that a force of 400 men" was working upon the grade below Silverton, "pushing matters rapidly." This gave "very tangible hopes that the approach of the iron horse is not in the too distant future." On May 21, 1881, the *La Plata Miner* reported that railroad men, "who are supposed to know," say that the railroad will be completed "to Silverton by January 1, 1882."

The love affair briefly turned sour the previous August, when the newspaper accused the D&RG of trying to "kill" smelting plants in Silverton, because they would compete with Durango. Nothing was worse than a lover spurned! The *La Plata Miner* (August 13) accused Palmer and his friends of wanting to buy mines at a fraction of their true value. Why else would they "destroy the most successful smelting works in all southern Colorado?" With no local smelting works, the value of the mines went down, or so the newspaper argued. The editor also did his historic homework and blasted the railroad: "Does anyone know of a prosperous town or community" in Colorado, before the coming of the D&RG, "which the railroad had not tried to kill and destroy when it built through or near?" Animas City knew too well.

That tempest died. It was more exciting to realize that the grading crews were approaching Silverton. When the year ended, the D&RG was back in the paper's good graces.

The costly "high line" was a favorite photo and tourist stop.
(Courtesy: Strater Hotel)

Its arrival would "create a revolution" in the mining industry and "make Silverton a mining town second to none in the State." The fact that the San Juans had richer mines than any other section "of equal extent" would soon be "demonstrated to the world."

The first benefit came the next January, when the H. A. W. Tabor Pioneer Stage & Express Line started operating stages from Rockwood. Staging was now reduced to 20 miles.

It was also encouraging that Colorado's premier silver mining man, Horace Tabor, invested in the San Juans. He also owned several San Juan mines and "where the big fish go, the small fry all follow." Denver's *Rocky Mountain News* said that southwestern Colorado was fortunate that a man of Tabor's "energy, ability, and resources" took such a "deep interest" in that section. The investors were coming. The year 1882 looked like a very promising one. Still, folks worried, because so much depended on railroad connections.

Anxiety gripped Silvertonians that winter of 1881–82.

The train seemed so close, yet, in many ways, so far away. The D&RG did not appear to measure up to their expectations, despite all it did. San Juaners had wanted the iron horse several years ago. Still, it had not arrived.

The D&RG was coming, but it faced many engineering and construction problems. Fortunately, wintry weather held off into the late fall and spring came early. Even so, the obstacles loomed large. If surveyors had to hang over the canyon walls, so did workers to blast the ledge north of Rockwood that would allow the train to drop down into the Animas Canyon. Now called the high line, it is the most spectacular, scary part of the Durango/ Silverton line. Its cost, it was rumored, was $1,000 a foot to build. Nay-sayers predicted only doom for Palmer and his railroad. They felt certain Palmer and his investors would never recover their investment.

Meanwhile, Silvertonians and San Juaners watched and waited, not always patiently. They were cheered in February 1882, when construction engineer Thomas Wigglesworth reported that all the bridges were nearly finished and grading would resume "at once." About time, some folks muttered, for grading now almost extended to Silverton.

By March, 200 men were reported working, a number that jumped to 500 later in the month. The *San Juan Herald* encouraged its readers on March 16, "Keep up your courage, boys; the good time's coming right along." A month later, the paper reported the railroad would be completed by the middle of June. Again, the paper returned to a familiar theme, while defending "Colorado's baby railroad." "The difficult problem of our prosperity will then be solved, and we will then have to thank the enterprise and pluck of the much maligned narrow gauge."

In May, both Silverton papers reported the railroad drawing closer by the week. It just did not arrive. Then, Wigglesworth reappeared to negotiate a site for the depot and railroad yards. When it was announced that the D&RG had settled on land nearly a mile and a half from downtown

Silverton, dismay set it again. The *Herald* (June 15) bristled. "The railroad depot should be located near enough to the business part of town to be easy to reach at all times." The paper only hoped the railroad would agree upon the favorable terms, "without further delay." If it were not one thing, it always seemed it was something else!

Still, no train had reached Silverton; at least the grade had finally been completed. Even if the D&RG had not arrived, its advertisements had sprouted. On May 11, the *San Juan Herald* carried this one promoting the railroad: "The direct and popular Rocky Mountain Route. This line presents to Tourists and Invalids the best route to the leading mountain resorts." It then went on to list some popular mineral springs (Manitou, Poncha, and Pagosa, for example) and scenic sites that the trains could reach. Interestingly, the "cliff dwellings and Aztec ruins" were included, foreshadowing the later tourist rush. Tourism and health seekers were not what Silvertonians awaited. They perused the

The Durango depot and round house were right across the river from the smelter. (Courtesy: Author)

42

advertisement and read, "Open to Durango Stage connections." That was *not* what disgusted Silvertonians wanted to read.

Then came the great day. The *La Plata Miner* (July 1) excitedly wrote that the whistle of a D&RG locomotive had been "distinctly heard in Silverton for the first time Tuesday evening, June 27." A big July 4 celebration was planned, heralding the nation's birth and the arrival of the Rio Grande. Silvertonians and visitors roundly celebrated the fourth, but, alas no train. The *Herald*'s issue of the thirteenth said that the bridge across Mineral Creek was finally completed. That overcame the last major obstacle. The D&RG had arrived, "even though," the *Miner* noted two days later, "all work is not yet completed."

"We will help the railroad, and the railroad will help us. That's about the size of it," crowed the *Herald* at last; the long wait was over. Silverton, the "Gem of the Rockies," the "Queen of the Silver Land," finally had its rail connections. Silvertonians proudly noted that their train arrived at 12:40 and left at 2:15.

The *Herald* also proudly noted that other newspapers hailed the completion of the San Juan extension. Silverton's day had arrived! The new *Denver Mercury* stated, "it opens to the tourist some of the most delightful scenery in America." Del Norte's *Prospector* believed now that Durango's coal and Silverton's ores would make a combination, the "key to prosperity itself." Finally, the *Denver Republican* admired the effort of the D&RG in building the San Juan extension. The paper regarded that effort " as a marvel of modern engineering and railroad construction." They were all right.

Silverton basked in the publicity. In anticipation of the D&RG's arrival, the town had been booming. Not a "premature boom," both papers hastened to say, but one built on the town's strong economic base and the district's mineral richness. With three hundred buildings within the "corporation," two "excellent" hotels, a "fine church building," a school house with "all the modern improvements," and a large number of merchants adding additions to their stores, Silverton stood ready for visitor, investor, and settler alike. It claimed a population of 1,200, "when the boys are home."

George Raymond, who owned and edited both the *Herald* and the *Animas Forks Pioneer,* hailed the coming of the railroad as the savior for both communities. None of Silverton's satellite camps needed that help more than Animas Forks. High up in the mountains north of Silverton, at 11,200 feet, it awaited nearby railroad connections to bring prosperity, as dearly as did its larger and lower neighbor. So did Eureka, Howardsville, and the newly opening Red Mountain mines. All of them now were "not behind the times," but each longed for its own connections.

Despite the ecstasy of the moment, the *Miner* issued a warning. A couple of "lady fortune tellers were seen perambulating" the streets, and an occasional beggar of the "professional class may also be seen." Silverton had "heretofore been exempt from these parasites." The advent of the railroad, the paper cautioned, "may be expected to inflict us with increasing numbers" of them. Other western communities had found this to be true. Now, locks would have to be put on the doors.

Not seeing all gloom and despair, the *Miner* paid tribute to the moment and, at the same time, told its readers what they needed to do.

"So far, all that can be done by the outside world has been done, for by this medium it has been opened to us— what now remains is for us to do—to commence to make ourselves and make good our statements."

CHAPTER 6

Dreams Fulfilled

The D&RG had arrived. In the words of a popular song of the era, it was "the year of the jubilee." Silverton and its San Juan mining district now had all three ingredients needed for a mining boom—valuable ore deposits, the best transportation available, and financial resources for development. The last finally appeared, thanks to the railroad, which brought ease of travel for investors. Repeated local promotion also was paying off in rich dividends.

San Juan County's mining production figures showed the railroad's dramatic impact on mining. The dreams had become reality.

	Gold	Silver	Lead/Copper	Total
1880	$6,000	$13,342	$42,900	$62,242
1885	$40,000	$749,000	$217,500	$1,006,500
1895	$849,411	$1,231,394	$479,324	$2,560,129

The first year the county topped $1 million in production was 1885. The silver production figures become more startling when considering the collapsing price of the white metal, from $1.07 an ounce average in 1885 to 65 cents ten years later. That figure represented what was paid for refined silver, not what the miners received for the raw ore at the portals of their mines.

Regardless, the train had arrived. Considering all the turmoil in trying to get railroad connections, it was amazing, but understandable, how quickly the D&RG was taken for granted at both ends of the line. As its presence was established, less news about it appeared, unless there was something like a derailment or a rare wreck. For example, a perusal of Silverton's *San Juan,* in June 1886, found only a few comments, but they offer insights into impact and acceptance.

D&RG train on the Silverton run, 1880s. (Courtesy: Flora Downtain)

The clock in the depot "got tired of running," one article noted, so the "boys" posted an obituary on its dial. "Rest in Heaven. Peace to its ashes." No concern about any railroad vs. Silverton issue now—nor the depot's location that sat only three blocks from the business district.

Late in the month, a special three-section train arrived, bearing John Robinson's "big circus." "A large number of people" went to the depot to see it come in. The first section had twenty cars; the last section brought the animals. The D&RG later generously held up the afternoon train, "so a great many who came up on the train along the line to take in the show could return home the same day." Such an entertainment could not have appeared without the train. A few "undesirable" folks also arrived with the show, but there was only a brief mention, no editorial comment.

Even with the praise for holding the afternoon train, one complaint emerged during that month. The "poor management" of the company had allowed a section of the road east of Alamosa to be washed out, thus stopping the mails from coming.

City fathers in both towns had to resolve some railroad matters. Durango, for instance, passed an ordinance limiting the speed of engines and cars, "not to exceed four miles per hour." The D&RG was to "construct a suitable crossing at every street," repair the same, and keep a flagman on every crossing to caution the public "against danger." Such must have cheered pedestrians and others. Trains could not stand at an intersection for more than ten minutes. The locomotives also were continuously to ring a bell while in motion and passing through town. Whether or not the city rigidly enforced these ordinances may be questioned.

The railroad arrived with benefits and burdens. Neither town wanted to march back to the pre-railroad days. But they did want to be sure the blessings outweighed the problems.

By 1900, Silverton had not one train, but three, tapping almost all her tributary camps and mines. Two of them were thanks to Otto Mears, the small-of-stature man, but a transportation giant. He had built, as mentioned earlier, hundreds of miles of toll roads, including several of the first toll roads into the San Juans. Then he turned to narrow gauge railroads, with Silverton as his base.

The first one, the Silverton line (1887–88), went over Sheridan Pass into the Red Mountain district and the camps of Chattanooga, Red Mountain, and Ironton. Like the San Juan extension, it, too, was an engineering marvel, which included a famous turntable to overcome a particularly difficult grade and switchback. The eighteen miles of curves and climbs proved very vulnerable to winter weather. He had planned to go on to Ouray, down the Uncompahgre Canyon, but even Mears could not overcome that steep grade.

The Silverton Northern (1895–96) was Mears' second Silverton line. It easily reached Eureka, eight-and-a-half miles north and only 500 feet higher, then stopped. When Eureka and its mines came into prominence after 1900, Mears' foresight paid off.

Silverton, Gladstone & Northerly locomotive, Gold King. One of Silverton's three railroads. (Courtesy: Center of Southwest Studies)

Mears planned to go on to Animas Forks and over the mountains to Lake City; however, the times were not right. Finally, in 1904, the line reached Animas Forks, but too late for the camp and too late, unfortunately, for the Silverton Northern to be lucrative up there. Two thousand feet above Silverton and 12.5 miles north, it would have taken a miracle to make an extension to Animas Forks profitable. The line was hit by heavy snow and snowslides, and the mines failed to pan out profitably. Mears never did get to Lake City.

Mears did not build the third railroad, the Silverton, Gladstone and Northerly (1899). It ran up Cement Creek to the little camp of Gladstone and its Gold King and other mines. This was the shortest of the three lines, slightly more than 7 miles. Mears leased the line in 1910 and purchased it in 1915. Mears had completed his Silverton railroad system.

During this Silverton railroad-building frenzy, Mears also found time to build the Rio Grande Southern (1890–91), from Durango to Ridgway, to tap the Rico and Telluride mines along the way. He went 162 miles to reach Ouray, because it was impossible to go ten miles down the impassable Uncompahgre Canyon.

All these lines helped make the San Juans one of the country's and the world's greatest mining districts by the turn-of-the-century. And Mears also promoted tourism. His Silverton line was the last link in what became known as the "Circle Route" from Denver to Durango to Ouray, then back to Denver. The tourists saw spectacular scenery and mining towns, got to ride a stage from Ironton to Ouray, and were able to savor the "vanishing" West before it disappeared. The "Rainbow Route," as tourists also called the trip, became a popular tourist attraction until changing times and the automobile did it in.

Mears' system never gained independence from the Denver & Rio Grande. All of his trains tied into the larger line and remained basically feeder lines for it. In fact, the D&RG had bankrolled the Rio Grande Southern and took it over when Mears lost it to bankruptcy after 1893's national economic crash.

Eighteen-ninety-three proved a very bad year for Colorado, the country's number one silver producer. The declining price of silver was complicated by the worst depression the United States suffered in the nineteenth century. It hung on for years, some places not completely recovering until 1900. Silver's price did not bottom out until it hit the 40-cents-an-ounce range. The result meant disaster for Coloradans in general and silver miners in particular. A Colorado report of September left these descriptions: Rico's situation was "hopeless," Silverton's "dark," and Durango's and Telluride's "gloomy." Said a resident of San Juan County, "Our only hope is a favorable silver legislation, if that is knocked out, we go out with it."

At the time, it seemed no hope existed, but it did. They did not "go out with it"; the San Juans shifted to gold production and soared as never before. Mears never regained the RGS and almost lost some of his other lines. The D&RG,

Keeping the line open in the winter caused repeated problems. (Courtesy: Center of Southwest Studies)

with difficulty, weathered the hard times.

If that situation did not prove bad enough, running the Durango to Silverton line had its share of other problems. It could be deadly for the crews. In January 1897, for example, engineer W. H. Young was killed when his locomotive collided with a rock. The winter weather, snow slides, varying freight shipments, and seasonal passenger travel that bedeviled Mears also bedeviled the Silverton extension.

Alex Anderson was in charge of the day-to-day management of Mears' two lines, while Mears worked back east as president of the Mack Truck Company. Anderson wrote several revealing letters in 1898 about the condition of Mears' Silverton system. In June, he predicted that "the outlook for the Silverton railroad this season is not very good." The Red Mountain mines, once heavy silver producers, were "doing nothing," or under lease. Anderson said that he was "doing all work with one engine to keep expenses down to a minimum." In September, he sent a much more encouraging report on the Silverton Northern. Prospects "are good," especially with the Sunnyside mine constructing a mill at Eureka. Regarding the Silverton line, he remained much more pessimistic. "At present there is absolutely no outlook for business. I feel very much discouraged." Both railroads fed into the D&RG, hurting or helping their prospects and profits.

Anderson complained about snow, rails in need of repair, and freezing weather. "We accept vegetables only at the owner's risk because of loss by freezing." As it was, the lines did not run often during the winter. The D&RG did, unless snowslides blocked the line, sometimes for weeks at a time. If the locomotives could not "buck" them, the hard packed snow, ice, rocks, and trees had to be hand shoveled. The Animas River, too, could be capricious. Both the Silverton Northern and the D&RG suffered almost annual washouts in the spring and worried about floods other times. Tracks were damaged, bridges washed out. Repairs took time and cost money.

All four railroads got into disputes with miners about ore freight rates. It was almost a seasonal matter. Both sides wanted the best advantage to be weighed against the depressed silver prices and hard times.

The *Silverton Weekly Miner* (January 4, 1890) vigorously complained about the high freight rates "exacted by the railroad." The point of contention was that the D&RG charged $12 a car to ship it to Denver, far more than elsewhere. "The great drawback for our young mines," wrote one disgusted reporter. Mines operating "on a close margin" could not ship, but if the railroad would "reduce charges by $3 then owners would gladly send." "Time and time again," the D&RG promised, "an increase in business at the station" would mean the freight rate would be lowered. "Now is the time for them to take action."

Quite typically, a love/hate relationship entered the marriage of town and railroad. Everybody wanted the railroad but did not want to be monopolized by it. Rates seemed too high, scheduling wrong, and the company domineering.

Locomotive off the tracks. (Courtesy: Center of Southwest Studies)

It happened throughout the West. Durango already yearned for a "southern outlet" by another line to break the D&RG's strangle hold. As Durango booster, Richard McCloud, observed, Durango was thankful for what the railroad had done, "but we feel it can do a little better." Competition, he felt, was the answer.

From the D&RG's viewpoint, and Mears' as well, this seemed like "sour grapes." The railroad had plenty of problems to face and owed its stockholders a profit on their investment. It was not easy operating a line in the San Juans with weather problems. Mining did not provide the granite economic pillar some people imagined. As the old mining saying went, "you could not see beyond the pick in the end of the mine." It had been that way since the dawn of mining. The vicissitudes of the industry were well known, compounded by the plunging silver price of the 1880s and the depression of the 1890s. Promises and expectations did not turn a profit for miner or railroad.

Then, there were those nagging little problems, such as the time a Northern train hit a cow. Usually the owner claimed this to be a prize bovine, but Mears caught a lucky break that time. He settled for $30, "which is less than the appraised valuation."

Although the D&RG and its three feeder lines had little squabbles, generally they got along well. Mears wrote in March 1892, "relations with the D&RG are friendly and cordial." With a little boosting pride, he concluded, "our road (Silverton) brings in large revenue for the D&RG. In fact, it makes 250 miles of that company's track remunerative."

As the new century dawned, the San Juan extension passed its nineteenth birthday. It had never prospered as its builders dreamed, but it had helped to open the Silverton mining district. And it brought a measure of prosperity to both Silverton and Durango, fulfilled the dreams of the former, and given birth to the latter. Complaints had surfaced from both shipper and carrier, some justified, some more emotional. Already the Populist Party had made railroads one of its major whipping boys in the fight to prevent a takeover of America by giant business trusts. Voters everywhere could see railroads and feel their economic and political clout.

The question remained: Would the new century be any better for the Silverton extension and the D&RG?

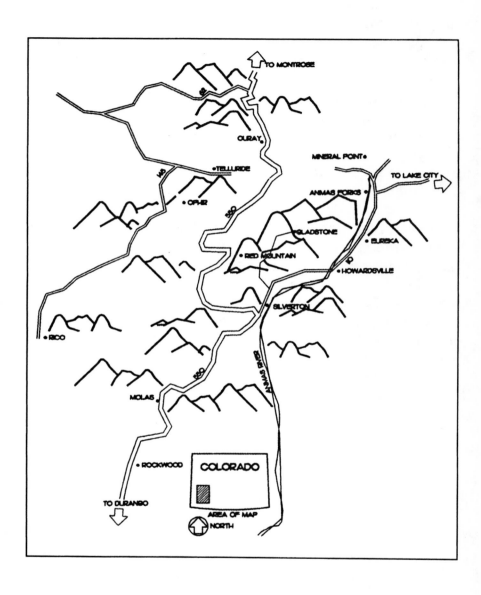

CHAPTER 7

New Century, Old Problems

The twentieth century proved to be, for the San Juan extension, years of profit and prosperity, then trials and tribulations, against the backdrop of changing times in the San Juans and Animas Valley. The Silverton district prospered through 1920, when it produced a record $3.6 million in gold, silver, copper, lead, and zinc. Then, the mining decline set in and, except for a few periods of recovery, the inevitable happened. There exist only a finite number of ounces or pounds of any metal in any district, and they, obviously, could not be replaced.

Mining would continue, and it still does. It has been going on for well over a century-and-a-quarter in the San Juans, one of the longest time spans of any American mining district. However, the district's high grade days peaked early in the twentieth century. Shipments of ore and mining supplies had remained a mainstay of the Denver & Rio Grande's Silverton branch. Now, it would have to find new sources of income or go the way of most Colorado narrow gauge lines and become memories of the past, a bygone era.

The railroad itself changed its name to reflect changed circumstances. After going through one of its periodic receiverships, and suffering a weakened financial condition, a group of bondholders purchased and reorganized it as the Denver and Rio Grande Western Railroad Company in 1920. It now ran all the way to Ogden, Utah, with branch lines in both states and soon the Moffat Tunnel would give it the long desired tunnel under the Continental Divide.

The reorganization meant little to the Silverton branch, other than a name change on the cars and locomotives. Already sections throughout the Rio Grande's trackage had been abandoned. Others would follow in the hard times of the depression locked 1930s and changing transportation needs of the post-World War II era.

All this lurked way into the future on the morning of the twentieth century. The Durango-to-Silverton train chugged along, as it had since 1882, facing all the old challenges. No difference there. It did have more contemporaries at the Durango station. The Rio Grande Southern was joined by the Rio Grande's "red apple" line (for the main freight item it carried) that went south to Aztec and Farmington, New Mexico, and a short spur line that tapped the coal mine and camp behind Perins' Peak, immediately west of town.

For Durango and Silverton folks, it continued as the main connective link between their communities. Their memories tell us much about a long ago era and its "love affair" with a railroad. Guy Emerson, who lived in Silverton in 1904–11, remembered one snowslide closure. "There was a tremendous amount of snow falling. We began to run low on things, but we didn't run as low as we thought we were, I guess." Groceries, meats, and other "goodies" began to be in short supply.

> I have to say that it was about thirty days before we had a train from there. That was a trying period. Many of the citizens had to volunteer to go down and shovel snow. They had Japanese workers come up there from Durango and that darn road—it was just snowslides on either side of the Animas Canyon. It was a very difficult situation. Otto Mears, as I remember, offered some of his equipment to the Rio Grande and they used that equipment working out of Silverton. We finally got the road open and everything was lovely.

Silverton, meanwhile, had been helped, when a pack train of jacks came in from Ouray with supplies. This proved neither the longest, nor the most severe, of the closures. Silverton learned to live with such trials.

Children like Ernest Hoffmann, who grew up in Silverton, remembered snow blockades differently—cer-

Five locomotives plowing through the canyon, about 1915. (Courtesy: La Plata County Historical Society)

tainly less threateningly. Once, with a slide near Silverton, a train would bring up newspapers and other "stuff" and leave it on the slide's south end, where it would be picked up in sleds and brought into Silverton by "ambitious" young boys. Townsfolk would greet them with cash, sometimes a dollar a copy. Starved for news from the outside world, they willingly paid such high prices.

Yet, there still remained some of the old complaints. The *Silverton Standard* (March 12, 1904) denounced the fact that the cost of freight for 6,000 lbs. from New York to the San Juans was $216. Compared with the ocean freight charge of $17 for the same poundage, that former amount seemed exorbitant. "The railroad charges were paid under protest," the article reported.

Nor did trains always run on time, or freight and mails come when expected. The railroad was not always to blame for such problems. Weather created just as much havoc as it had the previous decade, but it seemed now that people were more impatient. The litany of weather related problems included the familiar trials. Although many years offered no snow, floods, or any other complications, those years that did were long remembered.

In the winter of 1905, "old-timers remembered it as a bad year," snow and slides blocked the line from Elk Park to Silverton. A flash flood washed out part of the line above Elk Park in 1909. In 1916, "another worst year," slides blocked the line from February until mid-May. Two separate floods washed out tracks and bridges in 1927. For two months in 1928, snow closed the line. In 1932, the line closed from February into early May.

A rock slide in August 1951 blocked the tracks and created a small lake. That was followed by a three-month snow blockage. With the tracks located in a deep canyon above Rockwood, large amounts of snow accumulation did not generally threaten the line. Snowslides caused far more trouble. Most of them had names, with the Snowshed, Garfield, and Hunt slides being some of the worst offenders.

Nevertheless, they all paled when compared with the "flood of the century" in 1911. Folks back then called it that and they were proven right; it had not been equaled before, nor has it since. The flood raced down the canyon and valley in October, and the San Juan extension, at that time, represented Silverton's life line. Winter supplies were just starting to come in, and winter weather lurked around the corner. As people surveyed the mess in the aftermath of disaster, they knew something had to be done, and done quickly.

The October 6 *Durango Democrat* simply headlined it: WORST FLOOD THAT EVER VISITED THIS SECTION. Throughout the region, "nearly a hundred bridges are washed out." Railroad traffic "is demoralized." The Animas, joined by every other river flowing out of the San Juans, flooded track, farm, ranch, and city street. Water ran four feet deep through some streets in Durango. The newspaper felt "it is doubtful if half a million dollars" would cover the extent of the damages.

Locomotive 473 in the Durango Yards. (Courtesy: Center of Southwest Studies)

The *Democrat* reported that the D&RG lost track, "all the way down Animas Canyon." The Silverton line was not alone, "the D&RG and Southern suffer the most damage." The Denver & Rio Grande, none too financially strong, faced a crisis. It was known as "the sick man of Wall Street" for very good reasons. Equipment and lines had deteriorated throughout the system, it faced labor problems, and the company had sunk deeply in debt. Management had nearly run Colorado's no-longer-baby railroad into the ground. The D&RG had been down this road before and would again, but it did not need the added burden of this 1911 flood.

The Denver & Rio Grande turned to Otto Mears for help. He took locomotives, crews, and equipment from all three of his lines to push construction south from Silverton. The D&RG, meanwhile, moved northward from Durango. It took nearly two months, but it was finished before winter trapped the miners, townspeople, and others who planned to winter in the southern San Juans.

To reopen the line had cost the D&RG probably more

than it had profited from operations since the turn-of-the-century. Fortunately, Silverton's mines continued in a prosperous state and passenger traffic remained strong. Life breathed on the San Juan extension yet.

Despite such efforts by the D&RGW to keep running, Durango yearned for a southern outlet. Just as America entered World War I in 1917, this observation was made. A "broad gauge" connection to the south would open "up the vast resources" of this land and, finally, "yield its inhabitants a remunerative return." That sounded like the yearnings of a generation before.

World War I, meanwhile, affected the Durango-to-Silverton line. The United States government took over operation of railroads, large or small. The Rio Grande was paid for the use of its facilities and also received a $3 million grant to modernize its system and equipment. Not until the spring of 1920 did the government return the railroad to its owners. Some people thought the federal government should keep operating railroads throughout the country. As one person remarked, "the trains at least run on time."

The repairs and influx of money had long been needed. A 1914 report criticized the railroad for numerous things. Only one narrow gauge system, for example, was completely acceptable, the one over Marshall Pass. The rest were just safe enough to run trains "at some rate of speed." What speed that might be, the report did not say. Most of the cars and locomotives were out of date and had received only the scantiest maintenance since they were built. Silverton miners cheered when the report concluded by criticizing the railroad for "keeping its rates so high that low-grade mining could not be carried on at a profit."

The well-known engineer, John Stevens, who had been hired to make the inspection and report, accused the Rio Grande of being a quarter of a century behind the times. Many people from both communities applauded another observation. "During 40 years of intimate acquaintance with almost every section of the Great West, I have never known a section which has improved so little after being provided with transportation facilities."

The D&RGW was not without its own complaints, especially by the 1920s. San Juan's mining production started an erratic, downward path after the end of World War I in 1918. It, as mentioned earlier, would never recover, for any long period, the good seasons from before the war. Low-grade metal deposits and plunging prices did not help local miners. Silver, for instance, dropped to twenty-eight cents per ounce during some of the darkest days of the depression in 1932.

Railroad travel overall declined during these years, bringing further grief to the little line. These were *not* good times, and they did not "roar," as some writers have characterized the 1920s. Then came the crash of 1929 and a depression that certainly equaled the 1890s dark days in Colorado—and was the worst the whole country had ever witnessed.

If that were not bad enough, the automobile and truck already cut into train traffic, and public demands mounted for better roads. Another glimpse of future transportation appeared when the Durango Municipal airport "officially" opened in October 1929, only days before the stock market collapsed, setting off the depression. Both means of transportation spelled trouble for the Rio Grande system.

With the closing of the Durango smelter, the decline in coal and hard rock mining, and the near end of tourism, the 1930s spelled disaster for the Durango-to-Silverton line. Revenue waned alarmingly. It also did for the D&RGW. The "Dangerous and Rapidly Growing Worse," as it was nicknamed, went into bankruptcy and receivership. Some wags said, "Dead and Rapidly Growing Worse!" Neither bankruptcy nor receivership proved strangers to the company. In its history, they arrived with almost "timetable regularity." With the help of the federal government and New Deal subsidiaries, the railroad continued operations.

Plant and equipment improvements were made, including conversion to a diesel-powered line. More unprofitable trackage was abandoned. The San Juan extension did not

*Railroad buffs had discovered the line by the late
1940s. One used this for his Christmas card.*
(Courtesy: La Plata County Historical Society)

convert and became more isolated than ever. There existed
yet another reason for this isolation. Once, Silverton had
been the narrow gauge capital of Colorado, now only one
line remained. One by one, the three little lines had closed.
The Silverton, Gladstone & Northerly officially became part
of the Silverton Northern line after the closure of the Gold
King mine in 1922, the Silverton ended its run in 1922, and,
finally, the Silverton Northern quit in 1941.

By 1940, the D&RGW was back on profitable ground, a
reality that got better with the coming of World War II. Operating revenue jumped to 70 million by 1945, from 17 million a
decade before. A "new" Rio Grande emerged after the war.

Passenger and freight cars still went to Silverton, but the former was becoming more important. (Courtesy: Center of Southwest Studies)

All that was fine, but it made little impact on the Durango and Silverton line, which had managed to avoid abandonment but gained little else. Durango and Silverton, and the rest of the United States, entered the war in December 1941. Pearl Harbor, however, did not help their railroad that much. In fact, it threatened it. The government in late 1942 requisitioned narrow gauge equipment in Colorado and Wyoming to use in Alaska. Seven locomotives, for example, were taken from the D&RGW by the War Production Board. The Rio Grande Southern lost most of the needed equipment and suffered the indignity of being discussed for possible abandonment.

The local line was saved, thanks to pleas from the Durango Chamber of Commerce, La Plata and San Juan county commissioners, and other "influential citizens." Those "influential citizens" were, among others, Colorado's

"The last of the famous old narrow gauge railroads," proclaimed this 1950s post card. (Courtesy: Author)

senators, who pressured the government into issuing a "temporary stop order" to the army, as mentioned in the *Durango Weekly Herald,* March 4, 1943.

There might have been an increase in coal mining and "top secret" uranium mining, with the reopening and conversion of the old Durango smelter to a uranium mill, but the San Juan extension benefited little. Trucks hauled most of the coal and ore. Silverton's war related mines, those that produced war needed minerals (copper, lead, zinc), prospered some, producing most of what revenue the line received.

The "great depression," New Deal, and World War II ushered Colorado into a new world, one far removed from the halcyon days of mining and railroading. Despite nostalgic yearnings, there would be no going back.

Will Rogers might have written during his 1935 visit that "Durango [is] a beautiful little city, out of the way and glad of it." The San Juan extension could not live on that. "Being out of the way," as it most certainly was, offered no inducements. Rogers, incidentally, flew into and out of Durango. That told a great deal about the present, the future, and why Durango would not long be "out of the way."

CHAPTER 8

Hollywood Takes the Train

Hollywood discovered the Durango to Silverton train in the 1940s. The result was almost a decade of film making using all the local resources—the train, the Animas Valley, Durango and Silverton folks, and the San Juan Mountains. For some Durangoans, the late 1940s and 1950s generated the times of their lives, as they got to rub shoulders with movie stars and serve as extras in films. They never forgot those days.

Mr. and Mrs. Ed McDaniel remembered that era well during an interview. Retiring from the post office in 1953, Ed then "had a three-year hitch in the movies. Every fall, I would go out on movie location, *Around the World in Eighty Days, Night Passage,* and *These Thousand Hills.*" Ziporah McDaniel smiled and said, "Oh yeah, I forgot to tell you that, we're celebrities." Indeed, they were. She got out her album of photographs, which showed them in the movies.

Ken Periman loved to tell the story of how he served as Clark Gable's stand-in for a scene in *Across the Wide Missouri.* The situation was judged too dangerous to risk the star, so Ken stepped in. After running down a rocky hill, through aspen trees and brush, while being chased by Indians, he dove into a small pond, barely missing a large rock. He emerged from the water as Clark Gable. On a more tranquil note, Ken also remembered how Gable enjoyed local fishing.

Longtime railroad man, Alva Lyons, appeared in several movies, while working on the D&RGW's Silverton run. He especially recalled *Night Passage.*

"I was the conductor on the entire filming of that in Silverton, and where Tall Timbers [resort] is now, we had a spur out there. We had a lot of the local people [who] were dancing girls and other staff around the background crowd. We worked thirty days, I still have a picture of the movie

The Emma Sweeny all dressed up for A Ticket to Tomahawk.
(Courtesy: La Plata County Historical Society)

train and how it was made up, and we had twenty-three cars up the canyon with two engines, the passenger train, and the movie equipment—stock cars for the horses, box cars for the equipment, wardrobe, props—you never saw anything like it."

Hollywood came to Durango in a big way during those years. Movies had been made in and around the region since before World War I, but this time emerged as the golden age. A succession of films was partially, or totally, shot in the area. *Across the Wide Missouri,* a fur-trapping epic (1951) focused around Molas Lake, was the first "big" production. Then, Hollywood beheld the little narrow gauge train. Actually, it was found before Gable arrived.

And it proved almost love at first sight. Back in 1949, a relatively low budget musical-comedy, *A Ticket to Tomahawk,* had been shot on the mesa east of Durango and along the Durango to Silverton line. The train had been "discovered" before "Ticket." Producer Richard Bassler had commented that, while working in the area on an earlier movie, "we became intrigued by the narrow gauge running to Silverton and wanted to get it into that picture, but it simply didn't fit." Out of this came the idea for the setting of *Ticket to Tomahawk.* They selected the Durango area because of the still-operating railroad and the scenery. The writer of the script, Mary Loos, said, "the incredible Animas Canyon was the deciding factor to make the movie here. I'm glad because you get a beautiful look at a beautiful place that wouldn't be known without the train."

The shooting primarily took place on the mesa above town, where Fort Lewis College now stands. After much Hollywood effort, the train finally got across the mesa and miraculously ended up on the tracks chugging into Silverton. Following myriad adventures, comedy, a love story and danger, the story turned out in fine fashion. Dan Dailey, Anne Baxter, and others were the human stars, but the real star was the locomotive—the Emma Sweeny.

During filming in 1949 the *Durango Herald-Democrat* featured "Miss Sweeny" in an article about the movie.

" 'She' wears big [elk] antlers across the headlight and is no movie construction job. Emma Sweeny is Old Engine No. 20, a 38-ton job...which was born in 1889 in the Baldwin works and has been running ever since over hundreds of miles of narrow gauge tracks that thread together many mining towns in Colorado."

The article went on to picture what changes Hollywood made to the locomotive. Director Richard Sale described it: "We painted Emma Sweeney brightly throughout.... Her name is painted under each cab window in gold and her bell and whistle are bright brass. Her cowcatcher is ridiculously big."

The magical, musical, whimsical world of *Ticket to Tomahawk* portrays the mystic West at its most entertaining best. And, incidently, it also showed off Marilyn Monroe as a chorus girl in one of her earliest movies. While the movie never pretended to be more than a spoof, the train starred in some other films that took on more historic trappings, if not accuracy.

The 1952 film, *Denver and Rio Grande,* was filmed in several locations in Colorado, but the Durango and Silverton played a major part. The climax, a railroad collision, took place in the canyon. Two, about to be scrapped, seventy-year-old locomotives and a string of boxcars, loaded with 150 sticks of dynamite and fifty pounds of black powder, collided. The *Durango Herald-Democrat* covered the event. The crash jarred the ground for several hundred yards as the roar of exploding dynamite and steam rebounded from the hiss. Pieces of wood and steel shot high in the air above the smoke, sliced like shrapnel through the tops of trees and thudded like heavy hail over the entire clearing. The two engines and the cars gave up the ghost that day for a Hollywood special effect. Even so, despite their efforts, the camera crew failed to center the scene on the screen because of varying speeds of the two locomotives!

Night Passage (1957) starred the railroad and the region, along with Jimmy Stewart, Audie Murphy, and the supporting cast. The whole San Juans got in this one, including Silverton, Molas Lake, Red Mountain, and the Shenandoah-Dives mine, tram, and mill. In a typical "shoot 'em up," gun smoke and gallop western, Stewart saved the payroll and the railroad, got the girl, and killed the villain who happened to be his younger brother. The final shootout scene took place at the mill and tram, unusual in Hollywood films that did not often include mining scenes in their plots.

The coming of Hollywood made an impact beyond the filming. The Audie Murphy family, for instance, had a wonderful time. "It's really a vacation for us." The *Herald-News* reported the "Murphys have been fishing and they've visited the usual tourist attractions; just being here seems to delight them." The visits of Hollywood and the movies were doing more for Durango and Silverton than simply providing temporary jobs and entertainment. They were making both the towns, the train, and the region much more widely known. All this appeared to be for the better, especially, if one wanted the area to boom. The economy of the region was changing to a primary reliance on tourism.

The railroad played a more minor role in other westerns. In *Around the World in Eighty Days,* the D&RGW had to share the limelight with the La Plata Canyon spur line of the Rio Grande Southern. This 1956 spectacular was only partly made in southwestern Colorado, which was among the 252 shooting locations in thirteen countries. The cast briefly jumped aboard the Silverton train on their race to win the wager to go round the world in eighty days. The sequence from San Francisco to New York, however, was completely shot in the Durango area.

Ed and Zipporah McDaniel as extras in Around the World in Eighty Days. (Courtesy: La Plata County Historical Society)

The railroad appeared in cameo roles in *How the West Was Won* (1962) and *Butch Cassidy and the Sundance Kid* (1969). In the latter, the crew and actors were stunned when, during a holdup, the safe in the express car exploded with more force than expected. Too much powder had been placed in the car and the powerful explosion surprised everyone. "Cameramen had to stop filming so crew members could pick up the pieces of the car and throw them back into the camera's frame." The scene was shot south of town on Florida Mesa.

The golden age of Durango and the railroad's role in

Locomotives headed for a crash in Denver and Rio Grande. (Courtesy: Rochester Hotel)

Butch and Sundance leave the scene after a botched hold-up. (Courtesy: San Juan Historical Society)

movies was long gone by the time Butch and Sundance rode through the region. There would be much soul-searching as to the causes of this development, but no one had to look far to find out why.

The railroad repeatedly said "it was not in the entertainment business." The D&RGW worked with Hollywood, but not as enthusiastically as they once had. There only existed so many plots that could use the train and the scenery before the repetition and familiarity dulled the viewers' interest.

Other problems existed as well. Anne Baxter wrote that she spent "eight long weeks" in Durango filming *Ticket to Tomahawk*. Her acid comments provide an insight. "All of us lived in Durango at the Royal Motel, a euphemism, and ate at the local greasy spoon called the Chief Diner." Tourists and curious locals interfered with shooting scenes in Silverton and Durango, staring at the actors as if they were lodged in a zoo. Leading man Dan Dailey loathed the attention, finally being provoked into a fit of rage. "Suddenly, Dan danced up to a cluster, shoved his face viciously forward like a striking snake and hissed, 'They feed us at four!'"

There was a persistent rumor, based on some fact, that local merchants in the 1950s raised their prices, as motels their rates, when Hollywood arrived. Not until national motel chains with fixed prices appeared would Hollywood come back, and then only briefly, in the 1960s.

A combination of factors then ended the era, and Hollywood came and left, just as others had done before on the Durango and Silverton line. While understandable that folks would be curious about the film making, Hollywood did not help. An "eminently braless" Marilyn Monroe created commotion. Elaine Stewart posing for stills in downtown Durango did not improve matters either. "Cheesecake poses," the *Herald-News* called Stewart's photos.

Times were changing for the towns and their railroad. Mining declined rapidly in the 1950s and, with it, a decline in freight business. Silverton suffered. Oil and natural gas

Around the World in Eighty Days *briefly featured the train.* (Courtesy: Mike Todd Productions)

exploration and wells boomed Durango as never before, while agriculture played a less prominent role. Finally, a long threatening storm exploded over railroading. After World War II, the automobile almost totally replaced the train as the preferred means of travel, and the truck eroded the railroad's freight business. This impacted the D&RGW throughout its line, and every other railroad similarly. The result of all this changed the destiny of the line and its two towns.

Durango changed first. It quickly realized after the war that tourism offered the key to the future. "Come to Play You'll Want to Stay," trumpeted the Chamber of Commerce. Not everyone liked the idea, and some would have to be dragged kicking and screaming into the new world that stood ready to engulf them. How long would it be before the San Juan extension and Silverton joined the parade? The answers would shape the rest of the century for the narrow gauge.

Only Change Is Constant

World War II ended, and a new America emerged from the trial by fire. The days of Silverton's and the railroad's youth slipped far back into history. They were relics of another age, another era.

Mining continued, but only a few mines remained operating. With the completion of paving Highway 550 over Coal Bank and Molas passes, trucks now could deliver goods faster and, in many cases, cheaper than the railroad. That road and the automobile changed everything. It was the modern world exploding over Silverton. Silverton changed drastically. Gerald Swanson later explained,

"Good roads brought this about. Durango benefits from it, especially when mining is viable. Those big bucks go down the road. They buy everything down there. Today, Silverton has become nothing but a gift shop town. What services can you get here? You need glasses, you go to Durango or Ouray."

Even in the last great days of mining in the 1970s, miners lived in Montrose, Ouray, and Durango, but not many in Silverton. The Denver & Rio Grande Western continued operating, nonetheless. It carried fewer passengers and less freight. By the 1950s, only a mixed train remained, with both freight and passenger cars. Americans had fallen completely in love with the car and truck. Though not all Americans did—some still loved the steam locomotive train—not necessarily to travel on for any distance, but to enjoy for a while and to remember. These were the railroad buffs, and they did much to save the San Juan extension for history.

The D&RGW persisted in saying that it was not in the entertainment business. The railroad seemed to think that if the narrow gauge lines ignored passenger traffic, supporters would become discouraged and disappear. Abandonment, then, would be the logical move and, from the railroad's point of view, the "convenient end result." The Rio Grande was abandoning tracks throughout the system or converting to standard gauge, if the line proved valuable. Narrow gauge was losing out everywhere. The Silverton line, finally, became nearly all that was left.

The railroad might have been in favor of closing, but some of its employees on the Durango to Silverton run thought otherwise. The station agents, conductors, brakemen, engineers, and firemen

Myron Henry (shown here), Alva Lyons, and other railroad employees helped save the train. (Courtesy: Silverton Standard & the Miner)

worked to entice passengers on their own. In 1947, for example, nearly 3,500 people rode the train and, by 1953, that figure had jumped to over 12,000. A new era dawned.

Alva Lyons, designated conductor on the Silverton train was one of the prime movers. Lyons remembered those days when he carried passengers in the caboose, or in a freight car that had a baggage compartment, when there were no passenger cars. "That's the only train," Lyons reminisced, "that I ever knew of or any conductor who had a designated train he was the conductor of." In those early days of the late 1940s and early 1950s, it was a "homey" situation. "We always served coffee to any of the passengers in the caboose, that was the start of it, and I didn't actually start serving coffee in the big coffee pots until I was the conductor on the passenger train."

People came to ride the train—railroad buffs, those on a nostalgia trip back to yesterday, and folks who wanted to enjoy the spectacular scenery. Amos Cordova, who started working on the D&RGW in 1950, also recalled those days:

> The tourists as we know today didn't really start coming into this area until 1946 when World War II was over, and that's when the rail fans started getting out and about. Some of the rail fans discovered that this little train was still running, so I started working through them, through word of mouth.

Amos pointed out another factor to account for the new interest: "That time also was the time that diesels were beginning to come into the picture so steam was beginning to be taken off of a lot of major railroads."

Alva Lyons, Amos Cordova, and others helped arouse the local people to the growing importance of the train and the potential threat of the D&RGW's abandoning the Durango to Silverton line. Pressure built up to maintain the train, but the company resisted. Hearings, articles, public meetings, and genuine concern aroused people in both Durango and Silverton, as well as some of the "movers and shakers" in both communities. Thanks to all the effort, the train would not become another relic of yesteryear.

Meanwhile, the railroad continued to insist it was not in the sightseeing business, even if the Silverton branch remained viable only for that purpose. The Durango-to-Silverton was becoming isolated. Passenger service between Alamosa and Durango had been suspended back in January 1951, and, soon thereafter, there was talk of ending all service along the line. Over local protests, that would be achieved late in the decade. The San Juan extension now stood alone.

The D&RGW found itself in a dilemma. Some executives wanted to keep the line going, they "loved it." Others

Silverton historian, Allen Nossaman, Amos Cordova, and Alexis McKinney all did much to preserve the train. (Courtesy: Silverton Standard & the Miner)

wanted to let it go before excessive slides, or the cost of making extensive equipment and track replacements, took a firm bite out of the company's treasury.

In response to changing times, the D&RGW tried to sell the train to banker William White in order to set up a non-profit foundation to operate the line. Short-sightedly, both La Plata and San Juan counties protested, because they would lose a large tax revenue source. They failed to look ahead to see what tourism might bring in to more than replace lost revenues. The ensuing commotion and pressures caused the D&RGW to reconsider. It withdrew that offer, and other offers came to nothing. The company even tried to abandon the branch, but the Interstate Commerce Commission denied their request in May 1962. The commission observed that the line "serves a distinct public need" and contributed a "substantial profit to the applicant's system." The ICC agreed that the railroad could suspend operations each year between October 1 and June 1. Now the railroad

Finally, the Denver & Rio Grande started to promote its narrow gauge attraction. (Courtesy: Silverton Standard & the Miner)

had to decide what it planned to do. By that year (1962), with the train running 100 days, ridership topped 37,000. Cordova remembered those times.

"My wife and I were totally loading that train. We put people wherever we could, standing in between cars and stuff like that. Even the baggage car was used. We had a baggage car that we just crammed people into. There were no windows in it, but they wanted to ride so bad or bad enough, that they would take anything."

Finally, the D&RGW decided to tap the tourist bonanza on their doorstep. In 1963, the former assistant publisher of the *Denver Post*, Alexis McKinney, was sent to Durango to manage the Silverton branch.

He faced a multitude of problems, but he vigorously overcame them with calmness and a finely tuned sense of history and preservation. Steam would be king. There would not be modernization, meaning acquisition of diesels or other modern cars, of the line. Yet, that could be carried too far—some diehards wanted to recreate everything from the past. He drew the line. A proverb placed on his office wall said it all: "Beware, lest love of the antique lead to lamentation over progress."

The equipment did, however, have to be "modernized." For the first time since 1904, narrow gauge coaches were built in the Denver shops, with steel construction, not the old style. Locomotives were overhauled, and covered gondola cars arrived. Heavier steel rails replaced lighter older ones. Bridges were strengthened, and eventually replaced, so heavier locomotives could be used on the line. A baggage car was fitted out with snack bar equipment. "Unsightly" old telephone lines and a few trees disappeared from along the tracks in the Animas gorge to improve the travelers' views.

Equal time was spent to make the Durango depot area more hospitable, or, as it would become known, "Rio Grande Land." It had, at an earlier time, been one of Durango's Red Light districts and a small business area serving people on the south end of town. Over the years, it had deteriorated to something, as one person described it, "between skid row and honky tonk." That did not give the tourist the best image of the railroad or the town.

During the next three years, the pace was deliberate and carefully focused. The depot was spruced up, without altering its basic plan and facade. Amos Cordova described the changes: "We came in with Rio Grande Land, then we started to promote the narrow gauge passenger train a little bit more." With increased ridership, parking had become a major problem and concern. A parking lot across the tracks was cleared and opened, resolving for the moment what would continue to be a problem in the decades ahead.

The railroad quietly purchased the buildings around the depot on Main Avenue. These were leased to private individuals to operate with some tourist-oriented businesses. The General Palmer Hotel, restored and refurbished, for instance, replaced the older Savoy, described as a "third rate hotel." Some of the buildings, however, that had deteriorated beyond restoration were demolished. A few parking lots were thereby gained, but most of the vacant spaces would eventually be utilized to build the "modern" Victorian structures that dominate the depot district today.

The point of all this activity was threefold—to give the tourists more parking space, more shops to visit, and a better railroad attraction. These goals were paramount to the Rio Grande's intent. A happier, more satisfied tourist would likely spend more money and stay longer. Keeping her or him in Durango longer presented a benefit that could not be overlooked.

Silverton did not receive such bountiful blessings, although in truth the revival of the train meant more economically to that community than it did to Durango. Durango prospered from an oil and natural gas boom and the moving of Fort Lewis College into town. In response to the Silverton Chamber of Commerce's request, the D&RGW agreed to run the train into Silverton with the locomotive first, rather than following the "time consuming and unglamourous procedure of first turning it around at the wye and backing into town."

The rails were extended to Blair Street, which landed the tourists in the heart of the of the business district. Blair and Greene streets now became tourist-oriented, with gift shops, restaurants and anything that might tempt visitors. They had once been the business and entertainment center of the mining town, and now the impact of this "new" world would have its effect.

Not all suggestions were developed. A Durangoan, seeing that Silverton got its wish, suggested that the train be brought up the middle of Main Avenue, as far as the end of Sixth (now College). As was reported, the railroad "understandably did not encourage the idea." Tourism had swept the day! The conversion to passenger/tourist business was helped by the fact that freight traffic dwindled to nothing, despite the revival of mining at Silverton. For the first time since World War II, people did not have to worry about the train's future. After eighty years, the D&RGW actually was moved to state officially that "the railroad is in Durango to stay." It had realized that a profit, indeed a "tidy profit," could be turned by hauling tourists. From Durango to Silverton, a new focus carried the day.

Alexis McKinney would be in charge for less than three years, but during that time he set the foundation that has been built upon since. He proved that the railroad business and tourism need not be irreconcilable. McKinney also showed that history and natural wonders need not be compromised in the name of enjoyment and tourism. The "train that refused to die" would now be a "living memorial" to western railroad pioneers and railroading.

Regional and national advertisement kept pace with what was happening in Durango and Silverton. The "Matchless Travel Adventure" ran from June into September during the 1963 season. It left Durango at 9:15 a. m., arriving in Silverton by 12:40. The whistle sounded at 2:15 p.m. for the departure at 2:40 for the return trip. The "Journey to Yesterday on the Silverton" also stopped along the way, where flagged, and let off, or picked up, fishermen and hikers.

The decade of the sixties was one of growth and expansion. Then came a disaster that almost stopped the train, the flood of September 1970. While not quite the magnitude of the 1911 "flood of the century," it was bad enough in its own right. Some Durangoans thought it might be the end of the line for the train. Luckily, it was not.

Railroad vice president Amos Cordova recalled those days, when the damage was so great the railroad stopped running: "Mile wise there was probably about five or six total miles that were destroyed. But they were destroyed so bad that it washed away the road bed and left the rails and the ties hanging precariously, and because of that the railroad just couldn't run."

The D&RGW gave no thought to permanently abandoning the line, despite locals' fears. The company promised "to put the railroad back in operation one more time." This last deluge almost proved too much. The Rio Grande again seriously considered selling its narrow gauge line. For a while, it hesitated. Rumors spread, adding to local concerns.

When the train reopened, its popularity continued to grow. By the late 1970s, over 120,000 people rode it to

The flood of 1970 severely damaged the line. (Courtesy: Silverton Standard & the Miner)

Riding one of the parlor cars can be fun, despite the serious appearance of these folks. (Courtesy: Silverton Standard & the Miner)

Silverton. The changing railroad world beyond Durango and Silverton, plus the flood and the repair costs, pushed the D&RGW toward selling its isolated, tourist-oriented

By the late 1970s, the Durango to Silverton train had become a feature of southwestern Colorado. (Courtesy: Richard Gilbert)

line. The fact of increased ridership made the line more attractive to potential buyers, an added bonus for the Rio Grande. President Gale Aydelott, while reaffirming "we don't belong in the entertainment business," also called attention to the increased expenses for upkeep, insurance, and the like, which exceeded, the railroad claimed, profits. The return did not match the investment.

The railroad went up for sale, but not just to anybody. The buyer had to match the standards of operation, financial backing, and appreciation for the line's heritage that the D&RGW desired. By the 1980s, a potential buyer had been found; actually, he had been interested for several years. What were the possible ramifications if train ownership changed? Few local people, in either community, had seriously considered the possibility. They would now. The San Juan extension was about to enter a new phase in its history.

CHAPTER 10

A New Era

As mentioned in the last chapter, the search for a buyer started in the late seventies. "There were lots of them," recalled Amos Cordova, who had to show the property. Most wanted, however, to "buy now and pay later." The Rio Grande, on the other hand, wanted money "up front" and a guarantee that the new owner would appreciate the line's heritage and run it accordingly. Only one man, Florida businessman Charles Bradshaw, filled all the criteria.

Durango celebrated a year-long centennial in 1980–81, commemorating the town's founding and the arrival of the Denver & Rio Grande. In the midst of that celebration, March 25, 1981, the sale was announced. At both ends of the San Juan extension, the sale prompted concerns about what the future might bring. One thing it brought was a new name, the Durango & Silverton. After a hundred years, the Denver & Rio Grande finally retired from the narrow gauge railroad business.

Bradshaw promptly pledged to bring improvements, while maintaining the train's nineteenth-century charm. The most visible innovations included winter trains and an increased number of summer season trains. He also increased promotion and, despite a few glitches, it paid off. By the end of the 1985–86 train year, 177,000 passengers had ridden the Durango & Silverton.

He and his staff also worked hard to improve public relations. The end result proved positive, and improved community relations at both ends of the line resulted. Charles Bradshaw put to rest many of the concerns about what private ownership might do to the line. Nonetheless, with all his efforts, including some "new" equipment, the train faced what appeared to be more than its share of trials and troubles. Nor did all of his innovations work quite like he hoped they might.

Charles Bradshaw beside the short-lived Animas River Railway (diesel-powered) in 1988. (Courtesy: Durango Herald)

In February 1989, the railroad suffered a major setback when the roundhouse burned. Cordova remembered the day well:

> We had six locomotives in there in different phases of being repaired because that's our down time for repair of our locomotives. The fire department claimed the fire was approximately 2000 degrees Fahrenheit at the ceiling point. Of course, all the ceiling and roof fell on top of the six locomotives. They were all damaged from the top down; below the running boards of the locomotives, there's very little damage.

> We're talking about the most severe damage being caused in the cabs, where you have all the knobs and all the steam gauges, and all the clamping, and so forth. All that was totally destroyed. The locomotives

would be repaired and the roundhouse rebuilt. The spring season opened as usual.

The fire constituted only one problem the Durango & Silverton faced during those years. As professor Howard Hill warned his listeners in "Music Man," "Ya got trouble, folks, right here in River City." Trouble came from several directions and in several guises.

Back in the 1960s, Americans had discovered environmental issues. That changed life styles and attitudes remarkably quickly for many people. One need but ask the mining industry what an impact environmental advocates had. By the 1970s, some mining die-hards had bumper stickers on their trucks, "Ban Mining. Let the Bastards Freeze to Death in the Dark." More important locally, their attitudes greatly impacted mining in the Silverton area. Costs would go up and mining could not be done without one eye on the environment. The Durango & Silverton Railroad would not escape the long reach of the movement.

The issue of smoke and "quality of life" came to the forefront starting in the 1980s. People in south Durango, beyond the depot, objected to the smoke from the locomotives. The complaints particularly reflected the distress that came when smoke settled over their homes in the evenings and at night, while the boilers were kept hot for tomorrow's train trips. Even a few naive newcomers, north in the Animas Valley, objected to the smoke of passing trains. They had left smelly, smoggy cities to drop into what they considered a pristine Colorado mountain valley. Their sense of smell appeared acute, their understanding of local history and heritage bewildered.

This all led to letters to the editor and meetings in Durango. While the Environmental Protection Agency stated that the train smoke was within its clean air standards, neighbors looked about and disagreed. The issue has never been satisfactorily resolved for all parties, although negotiations continue.

Winter trains appeared for the first time in years in the 1980s.
(Courtesy: Silverton Standard & the Miner)

Financially more threatening to the Durango & Silverton was the question of forest and grass fires started by train sparks. These had happened in the past, but times had changed and now the "guilty" might have to pay for costs in extinguishing the blazes. The U.S. Forest Service and the railroad squared off over the Mitchell Lakes fire in July 1994. It burned 270 acres of national forest about fourteen miles north of Durango. The Forest and Justice departments alleged that a "coal-fire" locomotive ignited it and charged the railroad with "negligently causing the fire." They asked for reimbursement for firefighting costs, "allegedly $555,542."

The railroad countered by saying it had not "been negligent and that firefighting costs seemed unjustifiably high." Letters, demands, and conversations produced no solutions. The issue has "hung fire" ever since.

In the meantime, changes had come to the communities at each end of the track. The post–World War II boom came to an end in the mid-1980s. Tourism suffered a set-

A peaceful day at Durango, end of the line; this depot opened in 1882. (Courtesy: Glen Crandall)

back, then went into a period of ups and downs. The steady growth times of earlier years became a thing of the past.

In 1991, the last of the major Silverton mines, the Sunnyside, shut down. While smaller scale mining operations continue seasonally in the summer, the industry that built the community and sustained it for over a hundred years became part of its history and legend. Not that potential did not exist for future development. That always has kept mining going through good times and bad. But, for the present, Silverton had to rely solely on summer tourism for its main economic pillar.

There were jeep trails to travel, "ghost towns" to ponder, abandoned mines to "vandalize," the Old Hundred mine to visit, Silverton to explore, and the Shenandoah-Dives mill to tour—the heritage of mining remained strong. Those were wonderful and provided a grand opportunity to sample the vanished west. The train remained more important, however, to the town's financial well-being. Actually, the visitor had the wonderful, and unique, opportunity to see all the ingredients that developed and sustained mining—town, mine, mill, and train.

The train, and those few short summer major-visitor months, now became critical to Silverton's present and future. The steam-powered locomotive, and the passengers it brought, had become as important to the community as they had been back in 1882. As the saying goes, "what goes around, comes around!"

The Animas Valley changed, too. Development north of Durango reached all the way beyond Hermosa. Instead of farms and ranches, there were now homes, mobile home parks, a golf course, and a wave of urbanization highlighting what the train riders saw from their windows for the first dozen or so miles out of Durango. Not until the train finally pulled away from the valley and Highway 550 did the feel for the past start to take hold.

When management decided that the railroad could improve its attraction with a "modern" concept, the public thought otherwise. The idea of a diesel-operated railbus

The Silverton Brass Band poses before the depot. (Courtesy: Silverton Standard & the Miner)

Busy tourist season at Silverton. (Courtesy: Silverton Standard & the Miner)

from Rockwood to Elk Park seemed innovative. The summer railbus, however, never proved profitable. It ran for a few years in the late 1980s, initially with three trips each day, but the traveling public, and even the backpackers, wanted a steam train.

Perhaps, that failure says more about what passengers desired in the Durango & Silverton more than anything else. They wanted authenticity, not something that can be found elsewhere in a modern, more amusement park, train setting.

Actually, the success of the Durango-to-Silverton train encouraged the reopening of the only other remaining part of the old Durango to Alamosa line. The Antonito, Colorado-to-Chama, New Mexico segment carries passengers, also on a half-day or full-day trip. For the real train buff, a trip on both is a necessity. The two are not competitors, but rather partners, with the older line doing work on the equipment of the younger. Occasionally, they even borrow "stuff." The two lines, according to the Durango & Silverton, have a "good working relationship."

By the 1990s, the tourist boom of the previous two decades to southwestern Colorado had slowed and become more variable. Train travel plateaued, reflecting the times, but the Durango & Silverton kept operating. Winter runs to the

Cascade Canyon Wye were tried in the 1980s, discontinued, and brought back. A list of problems had been faced in over a decade of tribulations and accomplishments. Private ownership had kept the train running and promoted it with a new vigor.

As one of the chief regional tourist attractions, the railroad helped advertise the San Juans, Durango, and Silverton and bring people into the area. It still remained one of the most attractive and historically original of all American "tourist type" railroads. "We are considered the Cadillac and because of what we are people respect the operation we have and they consider us the number one train trip."

A triple header arrives in Baker's Park. (Courtesy: Silverton Standard & the Miner)

CHAPTER 11

Maintaining a Heritage

The Durango & Silverton Railroad long ago passed through its teenage years and, while not reaching old-age in railroad terms, it needs constant checkups and maintenance to keep it running. Slightly west of the depot are found those buildings and people vital to the train's continued operation. The watering and servicing areas for the locomotives, the car shop, turntable, the fifteen-stall roundhouse and machine shop area, and the skilled people who work there all assist in keeping the little train chugging back and forth to Silverton. So, too, do the crews that maintain the roadbed and plow the winter snow from the tracks. Times have not changed a great deal from 1882, when it all started.

Checking the birth dates of some locomotives and cars gives an indication of why constant upkeep is needed. The oldest business car operated by an American railroad, the "General William Jackson Palmer," was built in 1880 in the Denver & Rio Grande's shops in Denver. The veteran caboose on the line dates from 1881. The elder statesman among locomotives has a spry 1887 birth date. Three others date from 1902.

While the depot was built in 1881 and opened in January 1882, many of the maintenance shops are modern. The car shop, where the coaches are painted, for example, was constructed in 1982, on the site of the original D&RGW car shop. All the car restoration, building, and repair of rolling stock are done in this building.

Many narrow gauge turntables once existed, including the famous one on Mears' Silverton railroad. Now Durango has one of the very few remaining and operating. Built in 1923, it, too, replaced an earlier one, because larger locomotives were placed on the Durango-to-Silverton line. The turntable allows locomotives to be turned around and placed in the roundhouse for maintenance or storage.

Maintenance on the locomotives and cars is essential to keeping passenger service. (Courtesy: Durango & Silverton Narrow Gauge Railroad)

The original roundhouse, with its ten stalls for locomotives, was built in 1881 and burned on February 10, 1989, as mentioned earlier. Rebuilt, using part of the original walls, and opened the next February, it is the only narrow gauge roundhouse known to be constructed since 1906. The new roundhouse has eight storage stalls. There were none of this type in the old roundhouse. In this building, much of the repair and maintenance is accomplished that allows the locomotives to continue operating.

Each locomotive is inspected monthly; depending on wear and tear, each is serviced and repaired as needed. Certain parts of the engines are inspected monthly, semiannually, annually. Again, depending on wear and deterioration, the flues have to be changed, and that is when "you get into the very expensive part of the maintenance of locomotives because there are hundreds of tubes in there." This is an ongoing, year-round maintenance program. After all, loco-

Locomotives are occasionally purchased, sold, and sometimes traded. This one was part of a trade with Cumbres & Toltec line. (Courtesy: Durango & Silverton Narrow Gauge Railroad)

motives, and people as well, who have reached their "mature years," have parts that tend to wear out!

The machine shop repairs not only the rolling stock of the Durango & Silverton, but also on occasion, equipment belonging to other companies. It is the most modern and fully equipped narrow gauge shop in the country. There are twenty-seven machines inside to handle the various needs of an operating, narrow gauge railroad. As one visitor observed, "There's a lot of neat stuff in there." Ninety per cent of all the parts the Durango & Silverton needs are made in their own shops. "It's astounding the amount of work that's required and how they do it and what it takes for it to be done."

Speaking of their construction and repair shops, Amos Cordova explained. "Presently we are building or restoring any new equipment to our trains." He went on to say:

We are restoring cars for other people, doing outside work for other companies. We are the biggest one in this particular area that can do that. We have the

Inside the boiler at maintenance time. (Courtesy: Durango &
Silverton Narrow Gauge Railroad)

Track repair and maintenance is also vital to operations. (Courtesy: Silverton Standard & the Mine)

Rebuilding, repairing, and building cars occurs in the Durango yards. (Courtesy: Durango & Silverton Narrow Gauge Railroad)

facilities to do that now. Prior to the 1989 fire, we didn't have the facilities that we have now, of course. The fire, in this respect, actually benefited the railroad. The public can now tour the maintenance area to see what happens behind the scenes. Go beyond the normal visit to the train and depot and see what keeps it running. And, as a bonus, learn a bit of the history of the locomotives and the railroad.

As Cordova observed in December 1997, "When you get back and see what the maintenance people are doing back there, it's astounding the amount of work that's required and how they do it and what it takes for it to be done."

Like some of its neighbors, the depot, too, has changed over the years. An 1882 passenger would recognize the facade, but not the interior. That exterior would be the only sight that would make him or her feel at home while waiting for a train.

Passengers on one of the open cars. (Courtesy: Thomas Downing)

As the business of the railroad shifted to tourism, modifications needed to be made to match the changing times. At the start of the D&RGW's Rio Grande Land expansion in 1963, the depot's interior was drastically altered. Gone were the telegraph office, baggage room, and offices. The ticket office was expanded, and the depot's north end gutted. It became the present waiting room and gift shop. Restrooms were added inside; previously, they had been outside.

If nineteenth-century Durangoans returned, through a "time machine," to revisit their old hometown, they would recognize the depot and its railroad surroundings. During the summer, they would be amazed at how many trains departed from Durango. Even in the heyday of the D&RGW and Rio Grande Southern, not as many trains came in and out of Durango daily as they do today in peak tourist season.

Today's visitors can sample yesteryear. The smell, the cinders and smoke, are still here. The feel of the car, and the ride of an "honest to goodness real operating narrow gauge steam railroad" remain as they were in 1882. It is all

The railroad cheers on the Broncos. The year 1998 started out well for both the team and the train. (Courtesy: Durango Herald)

a part of a vanished America, a time lost many years ago. It is not an amusement park type of attraction, but an operating railroad that carries passengers and, occasionally a little light freight, between two communities tied together by iron railroad rails for over a century.

All this is possible because of the talent, time, dedication, and love for railroading of a legion of men and women, who work both in the background and with the public. They keep the railroad operating, not an easy proposition for the grande dame of American narrow gauge railroading. Without their dedication, the San Juan extension would be as much a part of history as its contemporaries, the Silverton, the Silverton Northern, and the Rio Grande Southern.

They are preserving a heritage, a glimpse into railroading and the railroads that opened and "conquered" the isolation and distance—the deserts, mountains, and "Big Sky" country we know as the American West. Mark Twain, who like many Americans of his generation had a love/hate affair with railroads, commented, "A railroad is like a lie—you have to keep building to it to make it stand." In order for the Durango & Silverton to keep operating, it has to be "built" upon, cherished, and, in a sense, loved. Twain would completely understand.

Mark Twain's experiences during his first trip to Europe inspired him to write, "travel and experience mar the grandest pictures and rob us of the most cherished traditions of our boyhood." Unlike poor Mark, traveling over the high line and into the Animas Canyon can rekindle, if for only a moment, a West of railroads and adventure and, perchance, our youth.

CHAPTER 12

The Nineteenth Century Greets the Twenty-first

As the decade of the 1990s neared the twenty-first century, rumors again emerged that the Durango & Silverton Narrow Gauge Railroad Company had been placed on the market. Indeed, that proved to be true. Finally, on March 17, 1997, it was announced that the First American Railways, Inc., an "entertainment-based passenger rail company," had acquired the line from Charles Bradshaw, Jr. The new owners, like the old, came from Florida.

The agreement stated that, for a price of approximately $15 million and shares of First American stock, the Bradshaw ownership, which began in 1981, ended. Bradshaw, who would be on the board of directors, told the media:

> We have great confidence that First American Railways will operate the railroad in the same manner as has been the practice for the past sixteen years. They have the commitment and demonstrated expertise that we believe will assure the continued success of the D&SNG.

The new company, based in Hollywood, Florida, owned more than the old San Juan extension. It was in the process of building a luxury, entertainment, "fun" train to run from Fort Lauderdale to Orlando.

The former owner might have great "confidence," but many Durango and Silverton locals did not, after a few press releases. The new owners could not have planned worse publicity. First came the announcement, within one day of the purchase, that the ticket prices would be raised. Adult round trip fares jumped from $42.70 to $49.10, a far cry from the 1880's $2.50. Actually, though, when considering a century's worth of inflation, that reflected very favorably.

As 1998 opened, the Denver Broncos won the Superbowl and their loyal Durango fans were given a free ride on the train. (Courtesy: Durango Herald)

The railroad had not increased fares for three years prior to 1997, while "overall expenses to operate the train have increased every year." "Traditionally, fare hikes had come about every three years," the company observed.

That might be, but the timing could have been much better. This fare increase came on the heels of a 1996 "down" tourist year for Durango. Opposition appeared, as usual, but did not go beyond muttering. The price increase was approved by the PUC, but damage had been done to the new owner's image.

Part of the increased revenue would be used for an innovative marketing campaign that First American planned to launch. The new company "wants to ride a tremendous resurgence" of interest in rail travel. "We're ecstatic. We've got the gem of the short-line passenger rail systems."

Then, the old question of damages for the 1994 fire, plus an additional smaller one in 1996 that charred about 25 acres in the Animas Canyon, came back into the news.

The Forest Service had never been paid, nor agreed to any compensation, by the Durango & Silverton. Thus, in July 1997, the U.S. Department of Justice filed a lawsuit against the railroad. That image of being unwilling to assume the environmental cost burden was compounded by the ongoing dispute with south Durango residents over smoke pollution. Neither issue painted the railroad in very good light and created emotional opposition.

To complicate matters, the town of Silverton and its residents became infuriated over a couple of issues. In June, the town and railroad skirmished over licensing terms for a photography enterprise that First American wanted to launch. The enterprise failed in Silverton, as it did in Durango, and left a bad taste in the mouths of locals. Said Silverton Town Administrator, Dave Erickson, "It's a real difficult situation to be working in. We certainly recognize the value of the train to Silverton. We also recognize the value of Silverton to the train. You can't hurt one without hurting the other."

This point of contention was quickly followed by another. One weekend in mid-July, the railroad had passengers board the last train of the day at a new spot, the depot. The "experiment" lasted three days. Train riders were told to walk four blocks to the train depot, rather than reboarding at the usual Blair and 12th streets. The question persisted, who was more upset—the tired, walking passengers or the merchants, who saw their customers' shopping time cut, as they trudged off to the depot? That time could not be replaced.

That decision to use the depot might have seemed strange and inconvenient to most, but a reason lurked in the minds of railroad officials: the potential of First American building its own "retail center near the depot on the outskirts of town." That posed a real threat to Silverton and its tourist economy. According to rumors—and the rumors always seem to swirl around this train—the company would build a "fake, miniature version of Silverton." This plan was heatedly denied by First American, but Silverton and the railroad seemed locked in disagreement. Silvertonians were also upset over late and canceled trains. Desperate not to see their major source of revenue cut by having the tourists shopping time cut, the locals complained loudly.

Communication between town and railroad deteriorated to a twentieth-century low. The mishandling of matters and threats by the railroad had only alienated folks. The situation was not helped by an innocent comment by the First American president, "I still believe Silverton can be the Williamsburg, Virginia of Western mining towns if they put their minds to it." Silvertonians had no intention of becoming another restored Williamsburg. Fortunately for all concerned, both sides wanted to do the best for the train and, it would seem, for the town. They appeared willing to work as partners for the future, despite a rocky start.

Meanwhile, the Florida train finally swung into operation in October. It promptly fell well short of projected passenger traffic. As a press release announced, "the company's revenue and cash flow from the operations of the Florida Fun-Train from October 15 have been materially below expectations." That again created all kinds of rumors in Durango and Silverton, including the potential failure of the Durango & Silverton, because its profits would go south to try to keep the Florida train running.

The rumor ended when it was learned that First American cannot "tap the Durango train's revenues to support its Florida operations because of written restrictions the company accepted when it acquired the D&SNG." The Durango train "is a totally separate operation. This train is not dependent on the parent company." The financial crisis, and poor public relations, did cause a shakeup in management, however. The chairman of First American promised that the Durango & Silverton "would emerge unscathed from its corporate parent's problems."

As 1998 opens, the train continues to run on its winter schedule. Plans are being made to better market the Durango & Silverton in the years ahead and improve relations with locals. The railroad also announced that it would continue to work to mitigate environmental impacts from coal burning in the Durango yards. It appears that the rocky first months of new ownership have finally calmed down. "We want to take steps to correct the mistakes made," announced Allen Harper, First American Railway's chairman and chief executive officer.

If that goal is achieved, then the Durango & Silverton should be in for a successful run into the twenty-first century. It has just gone through a period of tempest that reminds one of some of the local conflicts with its predecessor, the Denver & Rio Grande. That company had, at last, learned the importance of community relations. Now, its grandchild needed to learn, and retain, the same lesson. Only time will tell if that lesson has been mastered.

The Durango-to-Silverton train continues to run as it has since 1882. It has overcome a legion of difficulties and management mistakes to retain a flavor and spirit of a long ago time. As one Durangoan observed, "I think, in spite of whatever happens to the ownership, or whatever, I think this railroad will run in spite of itself."

Thomas Hornsby Ferril, Colorado's premier twentieth-century poet, perhaps summarized it best, when he wrote about railroading in his poem, "Cadetta-C&S." He caught the wonder of railroading for the young. And what is the Durango & Silverton, if it is not for the young, and the young-at-heart?

> The children have never ridden the train before,
> The children dream the train into the mountains,
> Chug of the smokestack blacking aspen catkins,
> They lean way out, they see the engineer
> Chasing the mountains off the track like deer,
> They taste the mountains tumbling through the windows,
> They smell the lightning singed by rainy roses,
> The river digs a tunnel under the train,
> Now it is gone,
> Now it is back again.

A Bibliographical Essay

Hopefully, the reader will now be interested in prospecting more into the fascinating history of southwestern Colorado railroads. Doris B. *Osterwald's Cinders & Smoke: A mile by mile guide for the Durango to Silverton narrow gauge trip* (Lakewood, various editions) is the place to start for the Durango and Silverton. See also her book, *Beyond the Third Rail with Monte Ballough and His Camera* (Lakewood, 1994). She has also written several books on the Cumbres and Toltec line from Antonito to Chama.

Robert G. Athearn's classic *Rebel of the Rockies: A History of the Denver and Rio Grande Western Railroad* (New Haven, 1962) gives the overview of the whole Rio Grande system. Jackson Thode's *George L. Bean and the Denver & Rio Grande* (Denver, 1986, 1989, two volumes) are a treasure of photographs and text. Robert E. Sloan and Carl A. Skowronski, *The Rainbow Route* (Denver, 1975) captures the various Silverton lines and Mallory Hope Ferrell, *The Silver San Juan: The Rio Grande Southern* (Boulder, 1973) and the ongoing multi-volume series. *RGS Story*, detail the history of the Rio Grande Southern.

The *Colorado Rail Annual*, published by the Colorado Railroad Museum in Golden since 1963, has articles on the Durango to Silverton and other local lines. So do the *Colorado Magazine* and *Colorado Heritage*, published by the Colorado Historical Society.

The third volume of Allen Nossaman's monumental study of Silverton and its mining, *Many More Mountains*, will get the train into town. For Durango see, Duane A. Smith *Rocky Mountain Boom Town* (Niwot, 1992), and its neighbor, *Silverton: A Quick History* (Fort Collins, 1996).

Savor, enjoy these additional books. As Abraham Lincoln wrote in 1862, "Fellow citizens, we cannot escape history." In the San Juans, like everywhere, it is all around you.

About the Author

Duane A. Smith is a Professor of History & Southwest Studies at Fort Lewis College in Durango where he has taught since 1964. Duane was named Colorado Professor of the Year in 1990. He received his PhD from the University of Colorado. His major areas of research and writing include Civil War History, Baseball, Mining, and Colorado. He is a "most important" Chicago Cub fan. Previous books published by FirstLight Publishing include *A Quick History of Silverton*.

Printed in the United States
131131LV00003B/64/P